SO-BXW-024

RETRIEVING TIMES

To Ainslie and Sue Gurney(?) and friends Affectionately Red

RETRIEVING TIMES

GRANVILLE AUSTIN

WRP

White
River
Press

Retrieving Times
Granville Austin

Copyright © 2008 by Granville Austin

Cover and interior design by Doug Lufkin, Lufkin Graphic Designs

Front cover photo by Steven J. Baskauf, Ph.D., Senior Lecturer, Vanderbilt University Department of Biological Sciences.

All rights reserved.

Published 2008 by White River Press
White River Press
PO Box 4624
White River Junction, Vermont 05001
www.WhiteRiverPress.com

ISBN: 978-1-935052-04-3

Library of Congress Cataloging-in-Publication data

Austin, Granville.
  Retrieving times / Granville Austin.
    p. cm.
  ISBN 978-1-935052-04-3
  1. Austin, Granville—Childhood and youth.
  2. Country life—Vermont—Norwich.
  3. Norwich (Vt.)—Biography. I. Title.
  CT275.A9245A3 2008
  974.3'65043092—dc22
  [B]
                                    2008029030

To Jack & Cathy Shepherd
Friends In Deed

CONTENTS

RETRIEVED TIMES

CHAPTER ONE

RETRIEVING TIMES

The Town of Norwich, Vermont, laid its spell on me in 1932 when I arrived at age five. It has never let go. Neither have I.

Retrieving my times in Norwich reminds me of this story. A man bought a retrieving dog and took it duck hunting. The dog neatly retrieved the ducks he shot, but in an unusual fashion. That evening he telephoned a friend and said, "John, will you come duck huntin' with me in the mawnin'? I got a mighty peculiar actin' dog." The two went hunting; the dog brought the prey as before, but he retrieved walking on the water. John considered the performance, turned to his friend, and said, "There ain't nothin' wrong with that dog 'ceptin' he cain't swim."

I have retrieved, as best I can, while keeping my feet dry, my times in Norwich. Individuals taught me. More, they and my surroundings learnd me, a mysterious process, somewhat like osmosis, dealt with in the final chapter. In effect I absorbed these times. Now, squeezing these absorptions and reducing the juice to concentrate, like sap from rock maples, I have become aware of much I was being learnd about the best of rural Vermont society in the Thirties and Forties.

The pieces that follow are about the presences—the individuals and stories and qualities—that surrounded me in Norwich, presences that live on as lively wraiths and give me pleasure to retrieve for myself and others. They may include the slight error or slip of memory. They may offer the occasional lesson but no moral. They are about my times, little about myself. They neither make nor follow a pattern. They are what I chose to write about. For me, my times at the time and since seemed a golden age. I little doubt that some contemporaries felt the drawbacks often associated with small towns: gossip, limited privacy, citizens' barely concealed ill-feelings, a few families feuding. Yet as I pierce the mists I think that Norwich compares well with our current national environment, replete as it is with greed, meanness, and deception.

My presences were companions young, older, and old; mentors (a term learned much later) or good examples; citizens and codgers and the tales they told about each other; fields and trees and excursions among them; the local history that became mine; and the conduct and standards then firm as town meetings grappled with matters like how to raise and collect taxes in the Depression when some folks couldn't pay them. That's a lot to hang onto, but, as Robert Frost said, it is no less than treason for "the heart of man...to accept the end of a love or a season."

I think it neither soupy nor overly romantic to talk about standards and ethics when its sister word, "values," has been debased by preachers and politicians. Values seems a hifalutin word, anyway, to describe Norwich's culture when individuals looked at themselves—somewhat less often than at others—with humor. Simplicity was not equated with either stupidity or idealism. Cynicism was neither abundant nor dead. I lived among a host of qualities: the decency possible where time moves slowly; the good sense of men and women who spend their lives in kitchen, field, barn, workshop, and schoolhouse; the ability of families with very limited incomes to live happily, and be dead straight in their dealings with others; the fellowship of a Protestant town honoring its Catholic sons killed in World War II; the skill and empathy of the teachers who taught us—they didn't learn us—the basics of English and arithmetic while keeping order among 25 pupils in two grades in one room. I also learned to fly-fish (not well), shoot (better), and ski. The few bitternesses, found in any town, I lazily ignored. This is partly hindsight, of course. Then I didn't think so analytically.

It's time to introduce you to Norwich. The town's charter was granted on July 4, 1761 for a settlement in the New Hampshire Grants (there being no Vermont then) by King George the Third. A precise location in the Grants was not specified. The general location was established by the governor of the royal colony of New Hampshire, Benning Wentworth, in Portsmouth, New Hampshire who reserved for himself some of the best timber in new townships. The King later sacked Governor Wentworth for speculation. For those of you from away who are as yet unaware, the town's name is pronounced Nor-witch, like the spelling on its charter, "Norwhich," not Nor-ich. Norwich village is situated west of the Connecticut River nearly half the distance from Massachusetts to Canada.

Like many Vermont towns, Norwich was born in Connecticut. Its first town meeting was held, a month after the granting of the charter, in Mansfield, Connecticut in William Waterman's inn with Eliezar Wales in the chair. Neither Wales nor Waterman ever settled in Norwich. Settlement began only in 1766, for security that far north was bad. The French and Indian Wars had ended only in 1763. Just four years earlier, Major Robert Rogers and his depleted force of Rangers, retreating after their destruction of the Indian village of St. Francis, had passed by Norwich's future location en route to Old Fort Number Four—later the site of Charlestown, New Hampshire. Their rafts were to be wrecked at Wilder Falls on the Connecticut river just south of Norwich.

Moreover, no site had been found for the village, despite the efforts of John Slafter who was cruising the forests seeking one. And when a site was decided upon, strong young men around Mansfield, Connecticut, were reluctant to go north; even the offer of $25 inducements failed to persuade. A site was selected five miles north of the Connecticut's junction with the White River. Surveyors began laying out roads (called highways) for wagons and sledges. They also divided the town's approximately 25 square miles (five miles on a side) into plots.

By 1770, development had become rapid. The first town meeting on the ground was held in 1768; crops were being harvested; a grist mill, a sawmill, and a tannery were operating; the first frame house was up. There was talk of building a religious meeting house.

Townspeople were essentially autonomous for the next 20 years. The charter gave the inhabitants the right to self-government. The politics of independence from Britain for the New Hampshire Grants swirled around the entire territory, heated up by the roistering Ethan Allen, bane of "Yorkers," Vermont nationalist, victor at the revolution-ary battle of Ticonderoga. Jacob Burton of Norwich helped draft Vermont's Declaration of Independence at the 1777 convention at Windsor, 20 miles down the Connecticut from Norwich. (Who chose to anglicize the French "le mont vert" to "Vermont" is unclear.) The document also established civil government for the state, which remained a de facto republic until Congress admitted it to the Union in 1791.

The town produced various eminences over the years, among them Captain Alden Partridge, who came from Norwich, graduated from West Point, became its superin-tendent, and established Norwich University in 1835—a military school that described itself as rigorously non-sectarian and dedicated to producing morally upright and patriotic citizens. After the Civil War, the university's barracks burned, its students and those from Dartmouth had taken to brawling, and the university was removed to Northfield, Vermont. G.A. Converse, another native, graduated from Norwich University and captained the USS Montgomery in the Spanish-American War. Admiral Dewey also was a Norwich University alumnus although not a native of the town. In the same war he gave us "You may fire when ready, Gridley."

The Georgian brick and wooden houses that the eminences built in the first half of the 19th century still grace Main Street. Across the way, when I arrived, was the Episcopal Church, the school (1898), the puritan simplicity of the White Church (1817, Congregational), and, farther along, the commercial heart of the village: Merrill's General Store, Gill's Store, purveyor of sundries and milkshakes, a small First National Store, and an inn. There were six hamlets at the town's fringes, most with colorful names: Root District, Beaver Meadow, New Boston, Jericho, Pompanoosuc (universally called Pompy), and Lewiston. Each, excepting Lewiston, had a one-room school, several a meeting house, most had a cluster of wooden houses, and only one a store. Lewiston, located right by the river on the road to Hanover, New Hampshire, had a railway station (Boston and Maine), a grist mill/grain store, a fuel oil distributor, a coal yard, and a cider mill. In my time, nearly a hundred miles of dirt road connected the six hamlets.

I travelled these on foot, by pony (Duke), bicycle, and car—after getting my license. A spider web of disused roads showed on the topographical map. Following these among trees and bushes growing to obliterate them, I saw stone walls, some still whole, others spilling their rocks left and right; barn foundations as true as when a family had put down the roots ill-fortune and time had pulled up; scrawny apple trees in forgotten orchards with trunks drilled into cribbage boards by sapsuckers. The wind and the deer and the partridges had reclaimed their own, leaving me contemplative and haunted and sad with the evidence of toils and joys gone by and the town's shrinking inwards.

Yet Thompson's *Gazetteer of Vermont*, using information compiled by the US Census Office in Washington, shows the town in 1880 to have been a hive of agricultural activity before successive generations left for the west and the cities and mills near Boston. The *Gazetteer* that year reported that the town had 700 milch cows, that it produced 73,432 pounds of butter, 37,388 pounds of wool, 17,000 dozen eggs, and 53,185 pounds of maple sugar. In my youth, there still were large dairy farms, maple syrup operations, vegetable truck gardens. The sole sheep of my acquaintance belonged to the farmer just below us, Fred Ammel. The ram butted me up the road when I baaa'd mockingly at him. The Brighams sold bushels of apples and, it was said, made cider brandy during Prohibition. Town meeting for decades had voted off and on to keep the town dry or to allow the sale of "malt and vinous beverages," ceasing its ambivalence with a wet vote in 1959. Until the end of national prohibition, several bootleggers assured that not all throats were parched.

Doctors from Mary Hitchcock Memorial Hospital and Dartmouth professors who chose the good life in Norwich hadn't yet driven real estate prices sky high as they are today. Wise, they had fitted into the town's common-man society, instead of keeping their distance. This was turnabout. Norwichers had welcomed the founding of Dartmouth in 1770 for it promised education for their children, jobs and markets for their elders. During the 1770s, ten citizens, several of them town fathers, deeded some 500 acres of land in Norwich to the college; and at the time there were also cash gifts, according to Dartmouth records. Nearby towns did the same.

This was the town and the society whose presences raised me. Going back to it in these pages, I think of Robert Frost going out to clean the pasture spring. "You come too," he said.

CHAPTER TWO

A PORTRAIT COME ALIVE

Will Bond's farm, 27 acres inherited from his father, was just up the road from our place, at the corner of Elm Street and Hopson Road, near enough for me to pester Will when I was small. He was in his late fifties, and I followed him around imagining I was doing a man's work. His tolerance seems to have been endless, for I spent enough time there for us to become familiar. He came to call this lively shadow, a hard ticket, whose meaning I never fathomed. "Granville, you're a hahd ticket." I don't remember when I began calling him Will, because it was contrary to Norwich protocol for someone so young to address a man so much his senior by his first name. In later years I may have been some use to him.

Sometime after Will died, I began to write about him. I never got beyond:

I knew him when he lived
Well enough to wish he hadn't died.
To passers by Bond's Place means just a man,
But I know better, and more.

And I do.

But Paul Sample did better. Artist-in-residence at Dartmouth College, he bought a field from Will Bond and built his house on it. Slowly, as befits sober men, the two became friends. Will came to like Sylvia Sample, too. He once said to me, "Sybie's a nice woman, but she's crazier than a bahn rat."

This friendship resulted in several sketches and drawings of Will over the years, a watercolor or two, and my favorite, an oil portrait of Will with his battered hat perched on frowsy hair above his lean face, weathered as a barn board. The cords in his throat stood out sharply, framing his Adam's apple. The straight-stemmed pipe hanging almost vertically from his lips partially concealed stained teeth. His loose trousers hung from faded yellow galluses over an equally faded plaid shirt, largely concealed by a dark jacket around his shoulders. Will appeared taller than he was. Even when seated, he appeared ready to get up and go right to the next job. His direct gaze, tolerant while skeptical, bespoke a calm man beholden to no one, who knew what he thought of himself and the world.

For several years Will's portrait hung in the sitting room of the Hanover Inn regarding the scene before him, maybe looking down, catching the eyes of those in the room. When he disappeared, removed to the oblivion of a vault in the college's art department, I wondered if Hanover's intelligentsia had decided that peasants should look up to them, not down upon them, and that Will, redolent of the barnyard, was overly genuine for their academic precincts.

The portrait's pipe was Will's companion when he was at rest. "Don't smoke while you're working," he advised me, during my early adventures with cigarettes. He had at least two pipes. One reposed on the tongue of his dump wagon, which he had backed into the wagon shed which made up one side of his three-sided barnyard, the other side being an equipment shed and opposite the barn. Near the pipe rested a tin of Prince Albert tobacco and matches. These were wooden not paper, which he called go-fer matches: light one and go fer another. One birthday I brought Will a tin of Dill's Best Sliced tobacco—my father's brand. Will accepted this with the surprise of a man unused to presents. He tried it in the next pipeful and said he liked it. The shed offered shade on hot days, and from the two graying round-backed chairs, one on each side of the tongue, we looked across the barnyard to the watering trough and the equipment shed and its huge kettle for scalding pigs. One day I asked to try the pipe. After a few puffs, earth and sky moved and I gave up, sacrificing pride for stability.

His second pipe sat on a small shelf behind the kitchen stove, where he could get it by reaching backwards from the rocking chair placed between the stove and the kitchen door. Will would light up in the kitchen, in the one room Mother, as he always called her, would allow him to smoke. Her name was Elizabeth, she had come from Canada, and he would chivvy her while she moved silently on thin legs at the stove and about her chores. He annoyed daughter

Helen by telling her that her cigarettes were made from bridge plank.

The wood stove had four rings for warming and cooking, an oven, and a reservoir at the back for ever-warm water. A cast iron pump with a curved handle—to draw water from their spring—was bolted to the counter so that its snout projected over the cast-iron sink. A drying rod for socks and such hung across two L-shaped hooks fixed in the low ceiling, just in front of the stove. One day when I was there, Mrs. Bond was trying out lard from a recently slaughtered pig.

Occasionally when I was sitting with Will, two of his sons would drop by, Charlie and Ed, both painters by trade. Charlie, as I heard, had been sent up during prohibition for making gin in the woods near the house. Bottled by Bond, he called it. I never figured out how Will felt about these sons. I never sensed closeness. His attitude towards daughter Helen seemed to me on the sharp side. She and her husband, Jimmy, and their young son, Donny, lived in the house and sometimes joined us in the kitchen. I thought Will contemptuous or mean toward Jimmy— who was likeable and had a good job at the college—and toward Donny, too. Later Jimmy moved out, and he and Helen divorced. I wonder now if Will hadn't caused those separations, although I doubt he'd intended to.

One day Ed and Charlie were swapping jokes and stories about mishaps involving ladders—buckets of paint spilled, ladders blown over in a wind, and really funny stuff—while getting haircuts in Walt and Ernie's Barber Shop in Hanover. I was in an adjoining chair. After they left, barber Walt said to barber Ernie, "don't you get awful sick of them ladder stories."

Will rarely talked about his past, and I regret I never prodded him to reminisce. But on a couple of occasions when we were sitting together, he did. "Back a long time ago," he began one day, "I useta run a livery stable behind the Norwich Inn. The hosses was in them sheds that is still there. One evenin' a fella walks in and wansta hire a buggy an borry a spade. He was respectable lookin', wore a wool suit of clothes. How long you want it for, I asks him. 'Jest overnight,' he says. So he pays in advance an off he goes. He brings the rig back the next day an goes off. Never a word. He come agin another time. I says nothin', but I got my suspicions that he was one of them grave robbers. I betcha he dug up some fellahs an they ended up on a mahble slab over to the medical school at the college."

Will could well have been right. Graves were robbed well into the 20th century to provide medical schools with bodies for the study of anatomy. But records of this occasion, if such it was, have eluded me. In 1895 a Dartmouth Medical School student stole the body of one Murdock from Hillside Cemetery, and was caught. Brief sensation. The medical school faculty paid the fine of $2,000 levied on him at the Windsor County Court House in Woodstock. The young man, John P. Gifford, later became noted for his good works in Randolph, Vermont, his home town, which included founding a hospital.

"You know," Will began another time, "I useta take care of your house when Caroline Farnham (from whom my parents had bought the place) went away for the winter. One day I was walkin' around, checkin', an I saw footprints in the snow goin' up to your kitchen door. I looked an that door'd bin jimmied open. God, wahnt I scairt. I went in an looked all over that house an couldn't find nothin' wrong or missin'. But you know that big front room with that four-poster bed. Well, they was the prints of two asses jest as plain in that bed. I nailed the kitchen door shut an putah new lock on it later. Come spring, Caroline come back. 'Everythin' all right, Will?' she says. Yes, Caroline, says I, but somebody had a boogerin pahty in your front room."

Caroline Bronson Farnam, whom I never met, has a special place in my memory. She left behind in her— our—house a tall secretary and within it a set of *The Temple Shakespeare.*

Will played a joke on me one day. Giving in to my plea to drive the team, he let me take the dump wagon up Elm Street. All was calm until he tickled the heels of the off-horse with a whip. Lummox's hooves grazed my nose, or it seemed that close. Will and Old Marshall, his hired man, cackled from their position behind me in the dump body. Will must have decided that I'd best go home with two intact jaws, so he put up the whip. Jim was the name of the near horse. Will thought him "clevah;" Lummox was "gormlin." I expect the term comes from the English, gormless, or awkward. Lummox was an indeterminate brown. No Percheron, he nevertheless had the feet of a plow horse and feathered fetlocks to match. Gormlin he may have been, but he was steady. When Will needed two hands, say to hold the handles of a plow, he'd knot the reins at the back of his neck and direct the Lummox or the team with gee and haw.

I never got mad at Will even when I nearly lost my nose (not "mad," Granville, my teacher would have instructed, "angry"), but I once got mad at his black dog. He'd gotten though the fence of the duck pond my father had made and stretched the drake's green and purple iridescent neck, and our hired man saw him carrying away the hen. Youngster though I was, I loaded a 22 pistol and took off up the road. I didn't find the dog, which I expect was lucky for both of us—for I intended to shoot him, and God knows what might have happened then.

Will's farming, when I was small, consisted of boarding a few saddle horses for neighbors, raising a few pigs on the manure pile under the barn, milking a few cows, and doing all the jobs that go with farming—caring for his own team, haying, and so on. I watched him butcher one of his cows in the slaughter house above the barn. He led the animal into the building, stunned it with a mighty whack between the eyes from the back of an axe, hauled its hind feet into the air with a hook, rope, and pulley, and cut its throat. The blood pulsed across the floor into a drain. When it had bled out, he let the carcass down, skinned it, and began cutting it up.

Taking a pig to the same fate, was when he showed me how you carry a live pig. This takes technique. One man holds the hind legs, the other the ears. If you hold the front legs, he'll bite you.

Winters, Will lumbered. He cut pine and hardwood in his woodlots both for the sawmill and for firewood. When cut, he'd skid out the long logs, chaining the butt ends to the sledge for the steaming horses to pull close to the road for a truck to reach. The four-foot lengths that he used for firewood were racked on the sledge and chained down, and brought near the house to be sawed and split when time allowed—for his own use and for sale. Will usually put a couple of forkfuls of hay on the sledge, outgoing, so the horses could munch while he cut or loaded wood. The logging roads Will cut to get at the trees, heavily marred by the horses and the five-inch-wide runners on the sledge, grew over to make fine trails for walks and ski touring. When I was small I stuck to these roads and those of earlier days. Wilderness lurked at their edges stoking caution in my imagination. I knew the way back home from the slope of the road: a pitch steeper than a team could pull logs up meant that homeward was behind me.

In my time, his market gardening provided a major portion of Will's income—and an even greater share after he sold some of his stock. Even then, the income couldn't have been much. His market operation was in two parts. One area of about four acres was planted in spinach and cabbage, which he harvested and sold in large lots. One evening, the story goes, Will telephoned Doc Jones and told him that if a young man came to him to get bird shot out of his ass, it really was rock salt and cloves. "The sono-fabitch has been stealin' my cabbages."

The other part he planted in an area south of his barn about thirty yards square. He had prepared the ground meticulously, plowing, harrowing, and smoothing it with a stone boat for so long that the soil was as fine as ground coffee. Each spring, with mathematical precision, he stretched strings the garden's length and maybe 15 inches apart to mark his rows. Below the strings he'd groove the earth for his carrot and beet seeds using the tip of his hoe handle. Beside them, in rows two feet apart, came peas and hill beans. Next came eating corn, usually Golden Bantam. I once knew the jingle for five kernels per hill: "One for the blackbird, one for the crow, one for the cutworm, and two to grow," I think it went. Beyond all this, near the edge of the garden where the vines had room to spread into the grass, he planted summer and winter squash and maybe a pumpkin or two.

When the beets and carrots had come up about four inches, Will thinned them. I can see him inching along on his butt pulling every other sprout. The carrot tops he fed to the pigs; the beet tops, still tender, he sold for greens. The few weeds that dared to appear, he scuffed down with a two-hand cultivator.

Will had a unity with his soil that I suppose he never thought about. Certainly, it was neither religious nor mystical. Down among the rows he seemed to be teasing the earth into productivity, and the garden was very productive. Fancifully, one might say that soil was his medium, its produce his meaning.

Harvesting continued through much of the summer. Because Will had staggered his plantings about a week apart, they ripened in stages. On any day he picked what was ready. Harvested peas and beans went into bushel baskets. Those for sale by the bushel to stores and restaurants in Hanover he weighed that way, 32 pounds a bushel for peas, as I recall, and maybe 30 for beans. Will sprinkled these with cold water—to keep them fresh, he said, winking at me because the damp also increased the baskets' weight. He'd load up the trunk of his old car with these, and in the back seat he'd put baskets from which he filled housewives' paper bags. My mother bought vegetables from him—carefully watching the scales—until our crops were ready. Will's always came first for his was early ground. Peas planted the first of May might yield for the traditional dinner of salmon and peas on the Fourth of July.

Sprinkling those baskets of peas and beans to make them a touch heavier was within Will's personal rules. We were relaxing beside the wagon tongue one day when a man drove a car into the barnyard. I knew from Will's tone

that he didn't like him. They talked for a while. Then the
man drove away. Will observed: "If a man cheats another
man, he's shahp. If he cheats me, he's crooked." Nor was
Will above mixing neighborliness with profit. When he
was boarding a horse for Dr. Lord, he showed me the bill
he intended to present to him. "Won't he holler when he
sees this," said Will, chuckling. Alex Laing, the librarian
at Dartmouth, lived near Will, and he asked him to mow
his field, taking the hay for pay. "Tain't worth cuttin', but
I'll cut it fer $1.25 an hour," Will said. So he got paid and
into the bargain kept the hay, which really was scrawny.

John Buchan admired Vermont, which he visited
when Governor General of Canada, and Vermonters, who
he likened to Scots. He said somewhere that a Scot would
imperil his immortal soul for a ha-penny bit but squan-
der pounds in hospitality. This was Will to the life. He'd
give you the shirt off his back, but dickerin' was something
else. He went at it gleefully.

Being around Will, I heard language that would
have shaken my mother. This takes some explaining. If
cussin' and swearin' are the same, and if they are defined
as what you say when you read about politicians or hit
your thumb with a hammer or reap the results of driving
your scythe blade into a nest of yellow jackets, then Will
swore no more than most men. Taking the Lord's name
in vain presented no problem, but it didn't characterize
his speech. I can't recall his using the F and similar words
common these days on sidewalks and in elegant drawing

rooms—of course, excluding those in Vermont. A horse or a man who was horny he called rhiny, derived, I expect, from randy. The barnyard furnished his vocabulary. He didn't often say dressing a field instead of manuring it, like our vegetable garden. He'd put the shit right to it. Refined folks would call his language earthy. Being conversational, it did not startle, nor did it please the ladies of the village. It was as much Will as his pipe and tobacco.

Will had a criterion for hiring. According to him, "a fahtin' hoss'll nevah tieah and a fahtin' man's the man to highah." I don't know if he applied this standard to Old Marshall who I first met splitting stove wood behind Will's house. This he did with wondrous skill, at least I thought so—easier than we'd cut cheese. Axe held halfway up the helve in his right hand, a billet of wood steadied on the chopping block with his left, he would tunk three times and four pieces would fall at his feet—one blow to split the billet in two, and a tunk on each of the halves to make four. A sizeable woodpile awaited his attention, but the unhurried rhythm never faltered. He exemplified the adage, "Don't let your head get ahead of your hands." Nevertheless, Old Marshall wasn't infallible. The ridge on his left thumb nail indicated a miss.

He lived just below our woodlot by the edge of Will's gravel pit in a shack with tarpaper nailed to the outside walls and newspapers tacked to the inside walls for insulation. Friendly, but not talkative, Old Marshall invited me in one day and showed me around. He had built a bed into a corner of the only room. There were a couple of chairs, a small table, shelves nailed against the wall for utensils and eatables, and an upright stove for cooking and heating. He told me the stove heated the place well even in winter, but he couldn't stoke it enough to last the night. Mornings were cold.

Marshall was a mystery to me. Where did he come from? Where did he go? All of a sudden, he just wasn't there. What did Will pay him? Not much I suspect. He ate his meals with the Bonds. I've been told that he spent his winters at a "County Farm" north of Norwich and appeared at Will's for planting and haying. My guess, now, is that Old Marshall—this was the Thirties, remember— was one of the last of a generation of itinerant older men who drifted as fancy and need took them, taking work as it suited them, trading comfort for independence.

A tumbled-down stone wall and a line of maples marked the boundary of our apple orchard and Will's lower field. A good fence it wasn't, but we were good neighbors. We helped each other. Often Will would give us fresh-cut rhubarb or heads of lettuce that didn't sell on a marketing trip. We'd protest and try to pay. "Take it, goddammit, I ain't usin' it," he'd say. We helped him, especially after Old Marshall moved on, for although Will still could mow and drive the wagon, he had no one to pitch the hay up to him while he built the load. Also, I cleaned stalls some days and tried to help with his gardening, but this couldn't have amounted to much.

We once helped him keep a grass fire away from his barn, beating it out with shovels. "Hope I cn do as much for you sometime," Will said.

One winter morning Will's chimney caught fire and Helen telephoned for help while the fire truck was coming. I grabbed a hand-held fire extinguisher—useless in the circumstances—and legged it up the road. The fire had died down by the time I arrived. Luckily the house hadn't caught. Chimney fires in the days before flue lining meant disaster for many a farmhouse, especially one far away from the firehouse. Going back home I discovered that my hair, wetted to comb before school, had frozen solid as a helmet. It was thirty below.

We came to depend on Will, and he did more for us than we for him. We had two saddle horses, a pasture and a paddock, but no hayfields and no haying equipment. We had a two-acre vegetable garden, but no plow or harrow or team to pull them. And we had no wagon to cart the manure from behind the barn to the garden. Every now and then Will presented us a bill. We dickered over several of these. One was so outlandishly high that I, about age 13, decided to make up a counter bill, whose total was a bit lower than Will's. He and I argued over this and he finally agreed to my figures, which may have been outlandish. I sealed the deal with a half-gallon of fishhouse punch (ingredients unremembered) left over from my parent's New Year's Eve party.

Will, as usual, plowed and harrowed our vegetable garden: on this particular day he and I dressed it with the help of Jim and Lummox and the dump wagon. From the manure pile behind the barn, the wagon had to go through our barnyard, through two sheds pierced by arches, turn right and go out the gravel driveway, between stone gate-posts, across Elm Street, and onto the tilled ground. After spreading a wagon load, we were heading to get another. I told Will to keep on, and I shucked my boots and grabbed a couple Fig Newtons from the kitchen. I was licking my chops when I rejoined Will back of the barn. He swore and asked if he didn't get anything. I suggested a beer, but he allowed he could use a real drink. "Don't make it moren half Sloans Linament," he ordered.

You old cuss, I said to myself, I'll fix you. I got a jelly tumbler, went to Dad's liquor cabinet and filled it up from the first three bottles at hand—maybe whiskey, gin, and apricot brandy. Will smacked his lips over the concoction and pronounced it not bad.

That afternoon, when Will reached the driveway, headed out with the last load, I asked him if he wanted another drink. "Trot right in an git it," he said, stopping the team. I asked if he wanted anything in it, soda or water. "Nope," he said, "I take my likker nekkid jest like I take my wimmin." So I prepared another jelly tumbler. He drank this down as I would a glass of milk, climbed to stand atop the wagon seat, cracked his whip, and yelled, "By Jesus, I better head for them gates while I can still see um." Horses, manure, and Will swayed on a dead run out the driveway and across the road into the garden. Had a car been coming...

As I grew older so did Will, somewhat to my sur-prise. His ailments in later years surely tried his courage and displayed his toughness. He had always been hardy. A few years before, when a mare he was boarding kicked him, breaking the double truss that protected his hernia, he didn't go to bed. He plowed that afternoon. He was Norwich's version of Ann Bradstreet, 17th-century Massachusetts poet, who recorded in her diary, "Churned butter in the morning, bore a son in the afternoon." Will's first long stay in Mary Hitchcock Hospital across the river in Hanover resulted from recurring prostate trouble. Soon after he came home—wan, but chipper and full of self-congratulation—he told me about it. "I was in that bed," he began, "an Doc Bowler come in. [Jack Bowler was a round jolly surgeon who understood the Vermonter he was dealing with.] 'Will,' he says, 'you're goin' to die.' Well, goddammit, I ain't says I. 'Well you are,' says he. Well I didn't. I wahnt comin' out of that hospital in no pine kimono." The operation did slow Will down, and each subsequent visit slowed him down further. He wasn't to lift. He couldn't plow.

These later illnesses cost him misery, and his friends misery, and a lot of money in the days when illness could send a family to the poor farm or put it on the town's char-ity dispensed by the overseer of the poor. Being so reduced would have killed Will. So he saved self and family by amputating the farm field by field, wood lot by wood lot. This must have hurt awfully, but he never complained. He sold the gravel pit where I sighted-in my rifle before deer season, the woodlot where I first saw him logging, the alder swamp where I saw my first green heron, and the marsh where I watched a marsh hawk glide flap glide flap glide, the white above his tail gleaming in the sun. Finally, the house and the barn were all that were left— and the barn his only so long as he lived—when it would go to Paul Sample, who had owned it since his original purchase. Then Mrs. Bond died.

For a couple of summers, Will maintained his vegetable garden, which someone plowed and tilled for him. But no horses chomped nor pigs grunted in the barn. The wagons and the tools in the sheds leaned back, not expecting to be called upon. Will sat wearily on the bench near the kitchen door, listening to August's cool cricket song while contemplating the daisies across the road, tanned by dust.

Will died in 1949. I didn't go to the funeral. No preacher would have done him justice. His grave is in Hillside Cemetery on a slope under a tall pine and a short maple, Lot 127 established by his father. I visited it wondering if it would be different from other graves. It wasn't. Mrs. Bond is also buried there.

CHAPTER THREE

CHINK

Chink and I became chums from proximity. He lived
an orchard and a field away—our orchard and Will Bond's
lower field—and we wore a path between his house and
mine. We walked Elm Street to school or detoured into
flanking woods and fields to collect last year's birds' nests
and flowers for pressing. When we were very young, and
it was summer, we built villages and farms on the sand
pile in the onetime pigpen that my father had cleaned out
and whitewashed before bringing in sand. We constructed
roads up hills and whined and snorted the trucks snaking
up them as they shifted gears on the way to our farms. I
still get a kick out of doing this in a grandson's sand box.

When older, we tramped the woods and Dartmouth
Outing Club trails. With others, we spent nights in DOC
cabins where porcupines had gnawed the doorsills, and
we alternated who got up first in winter to start the fire.
In Will Bond's woods, we once came upon a dilapidated
shed with flying squirrels living there. Winters we sledded; Chink did not ski. I wonder now if his folks couldn't
afford the gear. We chattered a lot and shared sandwiches,
cookies, and cocoa in each other's kitchens. The hottest

summer days we might make cold cocoa in our kitchen, fill beer bottles with it, and hide in a secret place in the barn. We chattered a lot, but I never knew how he became Chink; perhaps he didn't know. I was delighted later to read that Hemingway skied in Switzerland with a buddy called Chink.

The differences in our situations never came up in deed or word. We were boys together; words of friendship or affection would have embarrassed us. We didn't know the words "station" and "status," leave alone caste. My family was considerably better off than his. We lived in a big brick house with massive barns. He in a wood house— fronted by a wide porch and with three rooms on the ground floor: a parlor no one seemed to sit in, the senior LaPortes' bedroom, and a kitchen. Up narrow stairs, a bedroom ran between the gable ends of the house. Chink and his brothers, Jerry, Leo, and Paul slept on iron beds, lined up barracks fashion, with dust curls under them.

My father had worked in a bank in New York until the Depression drove him out. In Norwich, he took to wood-working and gardening, and my mother filled a room in the cellar with Mason jars of produce. She cleaned her own house, but the hired man's wife helped out in the kitchen and he outside. Our family was nominally Protestant, although we never darkened the door of the White Church (Congregational). The LaPortes were Roman Catholic and went to church in Lebanon, NH, Norwich village having no church for them in the early thirties.

Although my WASP mother restrained her appreciation of Jews, Negroes, and Catholics, she never remarked on Chink's religion, nor on my playing with him. Her sole remark to me was not to believe Chink if he said that his church was the first, something he never did.

Mrs. LaPorte was a thin, motherly woman, who enjoyed the boys' joshing and herded them gently. I never knew her other than as Mrs. LaPorte—and I addressed Frank as Mister. She was merry company in a faded dress, always ready to dry mittens in winter and make a jug of Kool Aid for us in summer. She painted pictures and made drawings. I liked them and think that today she'd be considered a first-rate primitive artist. Constant scrubbing, sewing clothes, and feeding big boys on small money kept her at home. The boys attributed their boils to bad diet and said they cured them by eating raisins, especially mother's raisin cookies. As Mrs. LaPorte grew older she seemed to turn simple. One day she told Chink and me in great detail how she had been in Hanover and gone into the Inn Coffee Shop. "They brought me porridge and a muffin and coffee and I put cream and sugar in the coffee and stirred it, just the way I do at home." Chink was saying to her, "Ma, Ma."

Frank LaPorte was an iceman in a time when many folks had real ice boxes. Chink and I rode with him the beginning of one long day to the ice plant in Lebanon, New Hampshire and watched the chain hoist lift thick posts of ice from their forms to be loaded onto his truck.

Knowing the needs of his customers, Mr. LaPorte at each stop would chop off the proper-sized chunk, grab it with his tongs, swing it onto the rubber apron covering his back, and lug it to the icebox—often sitting on the rear stoop, as did his. Iceboxes were wooden cabinets with two compartments. The top one had a metal lining with a drain pipe for the melt water. The ice went here, food in the bottom compartment.

Chink and I and the three brothers occasionally did things together. I recall one Fourth of July. Prior to the big day, Chink and I had our own noisy time. Firecrackers were not banned then and we bought "five inchers." Really five inches long and thicker than your thumb, with a covering of green cardboard, they made a very, very loud bang. On the big day, Paul, Leo, and Jerry had a rusty 45-quart milk can in the pasture across the road from their house. They put a small amount of carbide crystals into this—the same stuff used in miners' lamps—and then spit on the crystals. The moisture and the carbide produced gas. They set the lid on tight, and tossed lighted newspaper against a touch-hole they'd made with a hammer and a spike near the bottom of the can. The gas would explode with a whoof and the lid would go soaring. Repeat as directed. On such days, Leo made good root beer and ice cream.

Another time, Chink and I and Leo and Paul went swimming in Blood Brook in a hole a short walk from their house and ours. Willows thick on the bank overhung the stream, making the hole's 20 by 12 feet shady and cool, almost cozy. One day I was "swimming" the dead man's float, all I knew how to do—face down in the water, arms stretched in front of me, kicking my legs. I was happy watching the sun bright through the large and tiny bubbles rising as I drifted. I came to on the bank and learned I'd been drowning. Paul and Leo had fished me out. On reflection, I'm glad they did, but I hadn't been frightened; it had been a dreamy, pleasant experience.

Chink was rangy, bigger than I. I'd have been no match for him in a scrap. He had big hands and long, spatulate fingers. I still marvel that he drew well with them, even delicate work. I expect he inherited the skill from his mother. Every May, he won the American Legion school-poster contest for the Memorial Day poppy sale. "In Flanders Fields the Poppies Blow," was the yearly legend on the posters. In the village we peddled red paper poppies on wire stems wrapped in green crépe paper for whatever donations we could collect. Chink's poster designs, made with colored pencils, were bold and colorful, skillfully done—nothing like the childish attempts of us other sixth graders. We couldn't have produced a poppyish-looking poppy had our lives depended on it. His lettering was crisp and even. He taught me how to transform colored pencil lines into a solid color by rubbing them with a piece of blotting paper.

Memorial Day ceremonies culminated on the Sunday morning with a simple parade to the cemetery at the edge of the village. There were no fire engines, nor floats, nor fancy stuff. The band led the way, followed by war veterans in uniform. The last Civil War veteran in the village marched in 1933, I think. There were several who had fought in the Spanish-American War, and the men of World War One. At the tail of the column marched members of the American Legion and the poster makers and poppy sellers. At the cemetery, after trumpeted *Taps*, the uniformed men fired a three-round salute. The crash from their Krag rifles suddenly made the ceremony serious.

At Halloween, instead of cutting out black paper cats to paste onto orange paper, as most of us did—cats who would have shuddered at their portraits—Chink drew barns that looked like barns and black cats peeping around nearby corn shucks. He understood perspective and drew wonderful stone walls. We decorated the school room with corn shucks and pumpkins and red and yellow leaves.

Leo and Paul joined the navy in 1942 and were killed in the Pacific. During the war, the town made a flag with blue and gold stars and hung it at the front of the great room in the town hall. Who would unveil it? Citizens filled the hall for the ceremony. When all was still, Episcopalian Father Leslie Hodder, called "Frank," and Mr. Laporte, a Roman Catholic in the Protestant town, came forward to unveil the banner with the LaPorte sons' gold stars on it.

The town's Christmas Pageant was identical in spirit. Originally, each church had celebrated its own festival. The chaplain of the Grange, Glen Parker, had a better idea. Representatives of the churches gathered. They accepted the offer of Nick Jacobson, who was Jewish, to write the script. The procession began at Betty Booth's house on Elm Street, as she led her donkey with Peggy Ammel as Mary riding side-saddle. The donkey was known to like cookies. One story says that if he baulked, an Oreo might get him going. Arriving at Main Street, Al Foley, sometime town meeting moderator, read Caesar Augustus's decree that people should be registered and taxed. No longer should Nazareth be their destination. So the procession and townspeople headed up Main Street toward Bethlehem for Mary and Joseph to be registered, singing on the way to the Norwich Inn, where owner Borden Avery declared he had no room. Next, at the Grange Hall, gifts—ultimately destined for hospitals—were assembled and all proceeded to the hay-softened manger in Bethlehem, aka Glen Parker's barn. To this day, this manger, by deed, is part of Parker's former property no matter successive owners.

"Society" was a term foreign to Norwich. *The Hanover Gazette* (across the Connecticut) published no "society pages." Possession of a Ph.D. put no one on a pedestal. Only medicine men and women were addressed as doctor. A long family history in the town did bring prestige. Distinctions were noticed, but not observed as guides to conduct. In Merrill's Store, plumbers were distinguishable from professors, but citizens were expected to subscribe to the town's norm of equitableness, recognition of intrinsic worth. Perfection was not to be expected, but men and women, boys and girls, and the relations among them, were to be "true" in character, as the sills of a house, or posts, should be true—straight, level, upright, square with other elements in the construction. Other terms, with meanings and nuances hard to nail down, might be decency, good, or "doing what's right." If the standard was not tangible, it was implicitly recognized. Reputations were known. This was the atmosphere that cocooned Chink and me and guided the adults around us. I expect that other small rural towns during those years may have been similar. I just count the blessings fallen on me.

Chink and I became separated in high school. I can't recall why. Perhaps it was because he enlisted in the navy. [I waited till after I graduated to be drafted.] Or, because I spent my junior year of high school in Miami Beach, where the navy had stationed my father. Then I lost track of Chink. Much later I heard he was in Texas, working as a sculptor of grave monuments. Jerry opened a gas station/ garage in White River Junction, Vermont. I saw him once in a while and later was told he was doing pretty well.

CHAPTER FOUR

PIGWEED IS UBIQUITOUS

It sat at the back of the town common: brick, square, two stories, no frills, no nonsense, dominant, with Norwich Public School over the arched entrance in white letters on a black band.

It was my destination, even destiny, from Labor Day until mid-June from nine in the morning until four in the afternoon (Fridays until three thirty), for eight years, from ages six to fourteen.

From our federal-style brick house, notable especially for the three very tall white pine trees beside it, I followed Elm Street to school, walking on the road, for the town had no sidewalks. Down the hill on which we sledded, past Fred Ammel's dairy farm and the site of the tannery built about 1770, and then across the upslanting wooden bridge over Blood Brook. Here the dirt road became black-top. Urban Waterman's place came first on the left—he was a retired RFD postman—then Old Lady Kendall's weather-beaten house. Leon Merrill's well-painted house—he being the proprietor of the general store—was on the right at the top of the hill. Houses of doctors and professors and others continued toward the street's end. There, Joe Goodwin, squat and strong, had a car repair garage behind his house—white and square and one of the earliest built in town. Next to him lived white-haired Vic Bushway, father of Jean, dubbed "the bootleg queen of Vermont." The school was just across Main Street beyond the common's patchy grass.

Boys arrived early for whatever game was going. We smaller kids played marbles in front of the school, taking turns shooting with the side of our index finger at a soup-bowl sized depression we had scooped out in the dirt. The boy who got the final marble into the hole won that game and took the pot. Girls amused themselves.

As we boys gained stature—size and age—we graduated onto the common's expanse. In season we played scrub baseball, and occasionally a pickup team played Hanover grade school. We played tackle football with no equipment besides the ball. Bruises were few. When the town still had a baseball team it played on the common. Long hits passed over young maple trees into a field beyond and fielders had to chase them through long grass. When it turned cold enough, the firemen hitched a hose to a hydrant and over several nights sprayed layers of water on a corner of the common to make a skating rink. When it snowed, we kids shoveled it clear. Summer Friday evenings the town band serenaded from the gazebo-shaped bandstand in the common's corner opposite the skating rink.

At nine, the bell rang and eight grades headed through the double wooden doors—straggling, but not reluctant—to the first and second graders' room on the right and to the room for the third and fourth graders on the left. Fifth to eighth graders tramped up the broad, oiled-wood stairs, the fifth and sixth graders to the room on the right and the seventh and eighth graders to the left. When the time came to leave the ground floor and climb to the next two grades, we felt that we had left childhood behind and entered a grander world. Marion Cross presided over the seventh and eighth grades and was the head of the school. Zeus would have ranked no higher. She had been teaching in one-room rural schools and in Norwich for fifteen years before I had her in the seventh grade in 1940. These four rooms, plus a few smaller ones and the boys' and girls' toilets, constituted the school. To be excused to enter the toilets, we raised a hand showing one or two fingers to announce a distinction in our purpose, the necessity for which I have never understood.

The ladies in these four rooms did their best to teach us to speak properly. Not from suggestions, but through insistence: their eagle ears never missed a syllable. They pounced on errors, correcting us at once. Their persistence came not from prissiness or a stuffy view of language, which in our world as we grew older was robust, but from an uncomplicated awareness of what was right. They taught us, we learned; they didn't learn us. That was incorrect. English, including grammar, had been Miz Cross's favorite subject when in Johnson (Vermont) Normal School and her favorite subject to teach since then. We soon became aware of this.

For all the teachers, "ain't" headed their sin list—
perhaps because it was the commonest. The contraction
gained no legitimacy from daily usage. "Ain't" was speech
both wrong and sloppy. For them it was not suitable even
for the hayfield or the barn. Silent protests of "I ain't gonna
change my ways" would be met by firm, if unspoken, "you
surely will—at least in our hearing!"

Doubles were next in disfavor: double subjects, double
negatives, double adverbs, even double adjectives. "I ain't
got no pencil" and "I didn't hurt nobody" brought down
double disfavor, as did "it ain't hardly spring" and "he
didn't mean no hurt." We were not to say "not hardly"
and "we ain't got none." One double negative sticks in
my memory for being useful, if erroneous: "Don't never
do that again," typically said forcefully, rings in the ears.
It's an order to stop you in your tracks, or in mid-anything
else. Double adverbs evoked looks of disdain: "this is more
better"—or worse, "this is more betterer."

Double subjects came next in their disfavor. We were
not to say "Jimmy he did" but "Jimmy did". This is one of
many instances, it seems to me, in which correct speech
lacks colloquial speech's punch. "Jimmy he" puts Jimmy
right at the center of the action: "Jimmy he bagged a
paatridge" or "Jimmy he fell through the ice." The latter
is colder and wetter than if only Jimmy had fallen in.
The comma between Jimmy and he, even though silent,
added drama. In "Jimmy he busted his leg," the neglected
comma allowed Jimmy time to arrive on the scene and to

squeal with pain.

Teachers deplored double adjectives even when they were more descriptive than single ones, demonstrating again that proper speech has its limitations. "That big tall tree on the corner come down in the wind" summons up a bigger, taller tree, as well as a fiercer wind, than would "that big tree" or "that tall tree fell down." "That big and tall tree" is clumsy wording even if proper—besides, it denies the tree its grace. As you can tell, accuracy figured large in our observation of events. "Little small" frequently was said. For some reason, this evoked less opprobrium from on high. Perhaps because it is more expressive than either small or little, separately. Tiny was no substitute, and a word we rarely used, it being too small. Even bugs were small, not tiny. I still believe "little small" more descriptive than "very small," as in "he was a little small cuss"— human or animal.

Equally a cause for remonstrance was "me" as subject instead of object: "me and Charley." More often than not this became part of a triple subject: "me and Charley we went fishing." Properly, too, we were to say "it was those fellows," not "them fellers."

Verbs gave us unending struggle and "must have" brought our teachers to the brink of despair. Who, when talking as distinct from writing, fully articulates the help-ing verb "have?" We say "must of," as it usually is rendered in western stories or suchlike attempts to reproduce dia-lect speech. I think this is mistaken; it should be 'uve or 'uv, a contraction of have. It's taken me years to arrive at this brilliant conclusion. Anyway, must of, or uv, was out of bounds if teachers were listening. But I say it unrepentantly much of the time—and I'll bet that you do, too—using "have only" when I'm on my best behavior. And most of us contract it another way: using "shoulda" interchangeably with "should uv."

"Can" and "may" were troublesome verbs, and for me they still are. Try as I may (or can or do), I say can, mean-ing "I am able to do such and such," when I should be using may, as in "may I have the salt?" "Should" and "shall" fall into an equally dusky category. Except when I am thinking about it, I say "I will go"—which is the emphatic form, as we then were taught—rather than "I shall go," the simple future intention. Mixing up singular and plural verb forms was common: "they is"—contracted to "they's"—going or "we was going" instead of "they are" or "we were going." "They're going" is really just as easy to say, but it took time to get the hang of it.

We didn't get uptight about tenses, but our lady men-tors did. One of the correct forms easier to learn, which is not really a matter of tense, was that the dog "drowned" instead of "drownded." And a bitch was "spayed" not "spayeded." Anyway, in the classroom the word "bitch" would startle girls and evoke chuckles from boys. In use, the word rarely referred to dogs. "Himself" instead of "his-self" was a correction we didn't mind. "I seen her" at the dance was heard more often than "I saw her." "Seed" also

was heard: "I seed him in the post office." "Come" was used
more than "came": "I come home after dark." And "done"
was heard more than "did": "you done well to fix that roof
before winter." After a good performance of some kind, "you
done good"—never, except from a teacher, "you did well."
And "wahnt" instead of "wasn't": "he wahnt gonna go, but
he did." This would bring a teacher's double correction:
"wasn't, not wahnt, and going to, not gonna." "Gonna"
was a no-no. Still, it is hard to erase from my vocabulary.
It slides so smoothly off the tongue. We were admonished
to use "killed" not "kilt," although to me a man or a woodchuck seems deader if he's been kilt. "Been" often served
for "was": "I been there"—of course pronounced "bin." I
remember feeling justified, lifted by powers greater then
my own, when I read that Huck Finn didn't want to go to
Aunt Sally's because she'd civilize him; he couldn't stand
it: "I been there before"—bin as Huck would have said it.

This brings me to "good" and "well." How are you? How's
it going—or goin'? As a response, "well" just doesn't have the
oomph, it isn't as definitive as "good.' Neither does "fine," and
catch a Vermonter saying "I feel fine." No, good's the word.
It is solid; you can—not may—land on it with both feet. "I
feel good!" Conversely the reply might be "not so good" or
"poorly"—never "unwell." The same applies to occasions
when an adjective does better than the properly used adverb:
"turrible dry weather" is far drier than "terribly dry." "Turrible
dry" has menace. "The ears on the corn ain't fillin' out, the
well's near dry"—no "nearly" here. The water's lower than

that. As to wet, "it's wettern hell, field's so soggy I can't git a plow onto it."

Simpler than the complications of grammar, but exercising the teachers' vigilance and ours—when they insisted—were individual words that fell into columns marked acceptable and unacceptable. The unacceptable came in a wide variety. It was not "chimley" but "chimney." The word was to be spelled and said "library," although "liberry" was easier to say and to remember. The same with that uncomfortable "ru" in February; you really shivered when it was "Feberary." Although it was spelt "Wednesday," it was pronounced "Wendsday," and still is—a difference that did not seem logical, especially if we were wending our way on Wednesday. Things were "broken" not "busted," we were told, although here, again, "broken" sounds as though the object might be glued or somehow fixed. "Busted" connotes irretrievable, all "busted to hell-an-gone."

Teachers forbade profanity around the school, although it had a healthy existence in the world of workshop and farm. Adult language could be rough, but not so much as it is today, even among the educated. We youngsters did not use language common among youngsters these days, and rarely was such heard from adults. The F word, especially, had not come into common use. Adults might use shit as an expletive, but not frequently. As a product, manure typically was substituted. Spreading it on a field in spring was dressing the field. Among older boys, son-of-a-bitch was common off the playground. Knowing no different, as we would say, we didn't feel handicapped by these restrictions.

We were instructed about "mad" (insane) versus "angry." I wrote a letter to someone a while ago saying I was angry, but really I was mad. Also, teachers said, "individuals could be stupid, but only the truly dumb, were dumb." Unrepentant, I still say "that was a dumb move." Horses, or hosses, had bellies, humans had "stomachs." Will Bond didn't get kicked in the "belly" (the hell he didn't, broke his double hernia truss), but in the "stomach." Your father was "your father" not your "old man," and "how's your old woman" was impolite, and in certain circumstances might earn you a thick ear. "Old lady" for wife was acceptable. "Teats" was a sufficiently technical term to be acceptable speech—in the right context, of course. "Tits" were borderline, but OK if confined to animals. Yet care had to be exercised. One was not to say in front of a human female that "George was as useless as tits on a boar."

Reading to us one day in the sixth grade, Mrs. Cloud came across vulgar. She went to the dictionary. When she read out that persons belonging to the ordinary or common class in the community were vulgar, she snorted. "I am a common person, but I'm not vulgar," she said. This taught me to be wary of dictionaries. Another time she came across "ubiquitous." We asked the meaning. She said "everywhere." She thought a moment, and added, "pigweed is ubiquitous."

CHAPTER FIVE

Four Teachers

In Miz Cross's seventh and eighth grades, Leslie Dewing taught us music. She and Marion Cross were my first great teachers. Miz Cross will receive a chapter of her own later in this book. Mrs. Dewing was not on the staff, but a sort of adjunct teacher. She taught us about clefs, and how to read notes, about scales, keys, and modulations between them. We learned and sang a bit of Handel: "Where'er you walk, cool gales shall fan the glade; Trees where you sit shall crowd into a shade." This much I had remembered when I began writing this. The next two lines are equally lovely: "Where'er you tread, the blushing flowers shall rise, And all things flourish where'er you turn your eyes." The opera was *Semele*.

We sang a Welsh lament, which I remember, phonetically, as going like this: "The seagulls were calling wearily, drearily, Ahuru mayri du/ Come ye to me." We belted out the song of the *Grenadier Guards*: "Some talk of Alexander, And some of Hercules, Of Hector and Lysander, And such great names as these, There's none that can compare…, To the British Grenadiers."

We sang the sentimental lament of Churchill's Harrow: "Forty years on when afar and asunder/ Parted are those who are singing today." We were well acquainted with harrows, both disk and spring tooth, but that was it, and I expect that in 1935, few in Norwich had heard of Winston Churchill. His rise to fame was just beginning. It's a grand song.

We learned spirituals. Not just the better known ones like *Swing Low, Sweet Chariot*, but

> Ezekiel saw a wheel way in the middle of the air,
> A wheel in a wheel way in the middle of the air,
> Little wheel turned by faith,
> The big wheel turned by the grace of God,
> Wheel in a wheel...

Then there was *Little David, Play on Your Harp*. "Little David was a shepherd boy who killed Goliath and shouted for joy." The lines I liked best were those with a Vermontish refrain:

> Joshua was the son of Nun
> He never would quit till his work was done.

Doubtless there were church-goers among us, but we sang spirituals because they were rollicking and melodious.

For Mrs. Dewing we sang not badly and with joy, knowing little of what we were doing—sort of like enjoying a dessert although ignorant of its making. When we were lazy and sang poorly she would remind us of her pastor father in Canada. From the pulpit he would admonish his congregation, "The Lord loves good music—you'll be singing that hymn again."

Mrs. Dewing just was. She entered Miz Cross's room with the verve of a jack-in-the-box, clad in a tweed skirt, sweater, brown stockings and sensible shoes. Fiddle case under her arm, she greeted us with merry eyes that her thick-lensed glasses couldn't conceal. She would unsheathe her violin, tune it quickly, and play for us. I was told she was very good; I knew she was magical. No cobra would have been so mesmerized by a snake charmer's flute. As she played, her short bangs would quiver, and her body radiate music. Done, she would lower the violin, smile at us, and announce the learning for that day. I suppose she was middle-aged, but for me then and now she was ageless, and so were the days when she came to class.

Marion Cross and Leslie Dewing were the first teachers I had that proved that kids can learn anything. I suspect that neither of them set out to challenge us. That would have seemed a fancy notion. They simply knew that there were interesting and important things to learn, and they taught them to us.

In high school I had two similarly great teachers. Because Norwich, with its few students, couldn't afford a high school, Norwich kids had choices: go to a Vermont high school in White River Junction, five miles downriver, or north ten miles to Thetford Academy, or across the Connecticut River to Hanover, New Hampshire. This was much closer, and the town of Norwich paid the town of Hanover our tuition. I think all of us who continued school went to Hanover.

John Park taught English my junior year. Donald B. Grover taught math, and I think I had him for four years. Mr. Park had us reading books I wouldn't see again until well into college. We read, and he read to us: Countee Cullen and Langston Hughes, Wordsworth and Stephen Vincent Benet, Stephen Crane, Whitman, Oscar Wilde—no mention of Lord Douglas. We read *Macbeth* and *Hamlet* with, thanks to Park, some appreciation of the rhythm, the poetry, the meanings. This was a revelation after Mrs. Eulalia Blodgett's *Hamlet*, freshman year. A lady shaped like an oak, severely dressed, with steel-rimmed glasses, and smoothed-back hair of indeterminate color, she taught with the mien of an inquisition judge. Under her, Shakespeare suffered a drought. She parched each line. The play lacked passion, romance, agony. Where was Elsinore anyway? At least she made us memorize passages, which I regret I now have forgotten.

Mr. Park helped us live Hamlet's fraught indecision and Ophelia's anguish and shame at his treatment of her: how "get thee to a nunnery" could mean "get thee to a brothel," a term then infrequently used in a schoolroom, especially with girls present. He explained the symbolism of the previously meaningless flowers and herbs. We came to see that sound advice could come from a fussy old bird like Polonius. Above all, Mr. Park took us beyond the technicalities of iambs and pentameters to the excitement of Shakespeare's music.

Donald B. Grover strode across his classroom—Lincolnesque, his lanky frame in a black, chalk-dusted suit, bangs covering the top half of his forehead, the long face seldom at rest. "NEVER" he shouted in algebra class—and he chalked the word on the blackboard in letters four feet tall—"NEVER divide numbers connected by a plus or a minus sign." He reviewed eighth-grade arithmetic and led us through algebra to geometry to calculus to trigonometry to a smattering of spherical trig. So long as I was looking at him and he at me, I could grasp the mysteries, barely. Once his door had closed behind me, bewilderment returned.

We did our homework on yellow, eight-and-a-half by eleven sheets of paper, which he provided. Use lots of paper he advised; write big and label your numbers. If we believed we had correctly completed the problem he had set, we handed him the yellow sheet next morning. He would fold it the long way, bind it to our earlier efforts with a rubber band, and put it in his closet. If an individual did badly on a test, Mr. Grover exhumed his or her homework papers. If these showed slackness in the work or if you hadn't handed in many, you were in trouble. Before final exam time, Mr. Grover would set us a take-home problem extracted from the college boards. He asked us not to consult one another and said that whoever solved the problem need not take the final and would get an A in the course. No one cheated. The bulk of us faced the exam.

During the several days between the end of exams and school letting out, we continued to go to his classroom. Then, the math teacher flourished unrepressed as an actor. He read to us, striding about, his book in his left hand, extended before him like an opera singer in recital, his right arm gesticulating, his voice rising and falling with the rhythms of Scottish ballads. We heard how Sir Patrick Spens came to lie fifty fathoms deep.

A deadly storm is feared. Said a sailor:

> I saw the new moon late yestreen,
> Wi' the auld moon in her arm;
> And if we gang to sea, master,
> I fear we'll come to harm.

We heard of the wife's triumph in *Get Up and Bar the Door*. Busy with her chores the wife asks her husband to bar the door. He declines.

> They made a paction 'tween them twa
> They made it firm and sure,
> The first that spak' the foremost word
> Should rise and bar the door.

The husband did break the silence.

> Then up and startit our gudewife,
> Gied three skips on the floor;
> Gudeman, ye've spoken the foremost word,
> Get up and bar the door.

I think he loved us, frail students though most of us were. We reciprocated.

College at Dartmouth brought other teachers whose energy and acuity helped me learn beyond my ability. I was still a kid, and, well taught, kids can learn anything.

CHAPTER SIX

SEASONS

Vivaldi wrote of four seasons, and they have been noticed elsewhere. Norwich roads had three: plowing, mud, and dust. Maintenance and repair were in season year-round. Although roads commanded every inhabitant's attention, the selectmen and the road commissioner were responsible for their condition. Seasons had their folklore, stories sad and funny, stories of frustration and satisfaction. For me, at any age, they had their savor.

I have neglected deer and partridge seasons. The latter came in the fall. Grousing season came in March, town meeting time, the first Tuesday after the first Monday. Roads then were subjected to face-to-face, smile-to-smile, grumble-to-growl democracy.

Democracy and road conditions make a contentious mixture, helped along by town meeting's arrival in mud-time. Chances are there would be old or new snow on the ground and the wind raw as people rolled up at the town hall in mud-splashed cars and pickups. Mackinaws, heavy sweaters, galoshes, heavy boots, wool caps checkered black and red, or orange, from last deer season, were the fashion. A few men wore suits and fewer ladies, dresses.

School didn't keep so teachers could attend. Pupils were urged to attend.

On the steps of the hall, along with a last puff, the talk would go around: "Dammit, how's the milk truck goin' to git my milk aowt through that mud?" Or, "Last summer, they didn't scrape my rud good and the washboards shook the bolts outa my pickup." Or, from a housewife, "All right, but you fellas didn't have to wash your sheets twice to git the road dust offnum."

Attendees eschewing tobacco and preferring to be warmer would occupy the folding chairs inside the hall to await the moderator's gavel at ten. Elderly ladies could be seen reading the statistics in the Town Report, counting on their fingers the time elapsed between weddings and births—conveniently printed on facing pages. The meeting's business was printed in the "Warning" at the front of the "Annual Report of the Town Officers of the Town of Norwich, Vermont." Next to appear would be a list of town officials such a Treasurer, Overseer of the Poor, Surveyor of Wood and Lumber, Selectmen, Fence Viewers, and the appointed—not elected—Road Commissioner. Recently, looking at the Town Report for 1947, I found that I remembered 40 of the officials. For instance, H.H.Kew. A lean man in his sixties, he had delivered rural route mail, played the fiddle for square dances, represented the town in Montpelier, the state capital. He drove a Ford car whose voice I knew when he drove by our place on the way to his. He was listed as Cemetery Commissioner, two years. He and I sat on a hilltop in 1942 spotting planes to protect Vermont.

A road issue contentious at meetings before the war reappeared after it: should the town own a truck for road work. Such modernization was an awesome matter. The existing practice had the commissioner using his truck and billing the town for its time plus his own; other citizens with trucks would do the same. Were the town to buy a truck, someone with an eye to preventive maintenance would ask, "Where you goin' to keep that truck?" Dorrance Sargent regularly would reply, "You got all outdoahs, ain't ya?" An argument would follow about the effect on machinery left in the weather. Taking one side, truck partisans argued that if the town owned a truck it should build a garage to put it in. Another voice would say, "We ain't got the money for either one." Dorrance would assert that if the road commissioner drove his own truck he'd take better care of it, a commonly-owned truck would be neglected. Every March the meeting dug up these bones, gnawed them awhile, then dropped them.

Dorrance was a deliberate man. After he had a falling out with general store owner Leon Merrill (because Leon hadn't "treated him right") he vowed he'd never trade there again. So weekly he would drive his pickup from his place on the Turnpike to White River Junction for groceries, five miles down Route 5. Having absorbed Dorrance's deliberateness, the pickup didn't go very fast. Route 5 provided few opportunities to pass, what with its two lanes, curves, hills, and the town of Wilder to go through. So a line of ill-tempers would build behind Dorrance, horns sounded, and characterizations uttered about him and the truck.

Someone must have complained, and one day when Dorrance, unperturbed, was enroute, the state police pulled him over. The trooper civilly explained that it was common knowledge that Dorrance was a cautious driver and that the pickup had passed its prime. Yet people were complaining about being stuck behind him. The trooper hated to say it: "Mr. Sargent you got to retire this vehicle, get it off the road." Dorrance thought about it for a time and replied equally civilly that he'd have to replace the pickup with his "hoss and buggy." Retreating, the young trooper put on his cap and drove away in his cruiser.

A meeting after the war elected my father, returned from captaining a ship in the Pacific, one of the three town selectmen. After diligent homework, he developed a plan to buy a town dump truck and a big self-powered road grader and to build a garage to house them. Item 15 in the Warning for the 1948 town meeting asked if the town would vote to borrow $24,000 to buy land and road equipment and erect a building to house it. The meeting voted in favor, and the borrowed money was to be repaid at $2,000 yearly at no more than four percent interest. That summer I pushed wheel barrows of concrete, helping pour the garage's foundations on the New Boston Road. My father justified the grader as needed to widen roads for the growing town and to keep them up winter and summer. Done by the town, all this would be cheaper than by contracting the work, he claimed.

The road machine arrived on a flatcar to be unloaded at the depot in Lewiston. The company rep started it up, and he and the road commissioner drove it up Norwich Hill and into the village, stopping in front of Merrill's Store. Pedestrians and passing cars stopped, stores emptied to look at the bright yellow creature, at the long shallow arch of the frame, like a springing cat, at the big blade, the huge tires, and the cab sitting midway on the arch like a top hat. The rep looked nonchalant; my father wore the air of a successful midwife. Observers circled it, squinting speculatively, kicking the tires. How fast will she go? How much gas does she use? What'd she cost?, came the questions. As the grader drove out of the village, Harold Kingsbury, a big man with dark hair and a deep voice, said, "Well, we bought her. I hope she works." She did.

Fortunately for my father's career as a selectman, his success with the yellow road grader came the year before town meeting was confronted with the matter of the Pompy Bridge. This crossed the Pompanoosuc River (some say that to the Indians this meant "river of bright stones") five miles north of the village on Route 5. The state highway commission had condemned this venerable covered structure as unsafe, and an item in the Warning called for it to be taken down. My father advocated this as necessary to protect the town from a ruinous suit for damages. What, he asked, if a horse put a leg through the planking? Or, some wag asked, if events inside the bridge produced a birth, would the town be held liable? Vigorous debate ensued. Families from the hill farms on the south side protested that the bridge's absence would deny their children a short cut to the one-room school on the north side. Besides, the children would have to take the longer route across the new bridge that the state had built to straighten Route 5. "Cars on that new concrete bridge would be movin' almighty fast. Twant safe." Unable to decide, the meeting voted to postpone the matter. Mad, my father resigned on the spot—after placing a five dollar bill on the table—Vermont's fine for resigning office without due notice. My mother took him home.

A man was heard to say, "Murray Austin mustuv known he was goin' to resign or he never woulduv had five dollars in his pocket."

The typically combustible mixture of schools and roads produced especial anguish when the consolidation of the town's schools came up together at town meeting. Consolidation meant closing the outlying one-room schools and bringing the pupils into the village school. The rural families were loyal to the schools, and the village school seemed distant if not impersonal. Besides, the children would be herded into buses, and the mud seemed especially deep and gooey that spring. Mary Williams made the point about the roads, adding a lighter moment to the fraught atmosphere—likely not her intention. An expectant hush breathed through the hall as she rose to gain the Moderator's attention. "Yes, Mary," said Don Bartlett. "I hope," said Mary, "that you're to build one of them heeliocopter pads by the school." Shared looks of bemusement around the hall. "Yes, Mary?" asked Bartlett, unruffled. "Cause the way them rudds are this timeah year, that's the only way you'll git them kids to school." [For more about school consolidation, see Chapter Ten.]

My fascination with roads began when I was a small boy. If snow was falling heavily during the night, I would be awakened to the whining of a truck coming up our hill and the clanking on the frozen road of the skids under the plow. I would rush to a front window overlooking the road to watch the headlights glowing through the soft flakes. In the morning, the plow came by again. From our gate, I'd watch the snow curling ahead of the blade—like surf on a beach—clearing half the road, the other half to be cleared on the return trip. The dump body loaded with sand gave the truck weight for traction. A vee plow might come after a heavy snow, curling it left and right. Those blades stood nearly as high as the truck's cab. The yellow road grader with a bigger vee plow easily handled heavy snows.

Summer would bring another wondrous sight to our road—and me to watch it from the gate: Road Commissioner Ernest Fitzgerald honing our road. (I give his title initial capitals because commissioners had the most thankless job in town.) First the whining truck (when straining, they always whined) would creep closer pulling a red road scraper. On the steel platform above the horizontal blade, Mr. Fitzgerald turned vertical, large diameter steel wheels to adjust the blade's cant to crown the road. He scraped the khaki dirt on one side of the road to a cool damp brown, filling in potholes, smoothing the washboards. He graded a bit lower on the ditch side, a bit higher in the center to shed rain. Returning, he'd do the same for the other side. Slender, brown-faced, with parentheses of gravity from nose to chin, he'd look down at the boy and nod from his chariot, not breaking the silence of the boy's awe.

When use and rain had worn the road's surface down too far, Mr. Fitzgerald would be back. First the town added gravel. A line of three or more trucks—small by the standards of today's many-wheeled behemoths—would come up the hill, the lead one with its dump body tilted slightly and its tail gate set open a few inches to slide a fairly even layer of gravel onto the road. With his truck moving at a stately pace, the driver would hang out of the cab door, one hand on the steering wheel, one foot on the running board, looking back to check that the gravel was going on at the right thickness. Load finished, he'd jump into the cab, slam the door, bang the dump body back onto the frame, and head off to Day Barrett's gravel pit for another load—for which the town paid ten cents. The other trucks would repeat where their predecessors had left off.

Mr. Fitzgerald followed on the grader, smoothing where one truckload had ended and the next began. A hundred yards behind came the rear guard of stone pickers. Armed with narrow rakes with long curving tines, they'd hook egg-sized stones and flick them into the bushes along the road. When I was older I picked/flicked stones for thirty-five cents an hour. I liked the rhythm of it, the neat conclusive action, throwing stones for the public good. I also helped to load dump trucks in Barrett's pit. The dump bodies of those smaller trucks were lower to the ground, and their sides were lower, too, making loading easy— there were only human shovel-loaders. Shovels had had their points worn away by long use, and they sliced easily into the sandy gravel. With a rhythmical heave their contents went into the truck.

Ernest Fitzgerald headed a family of three boys and five girls, all of them above average, as Garrison Keillor would say, and respected in the town. I knew them all; two of the girls went to school with me. Mr. Fitzgerald was a man of talents. He had a fine baritone and when living in Lynn, Mass. and working in a shoe factory, he had played the piano and sung for silent films. RCA Victor had offered him a contract. When I rented a room above the family kitchen one summer, he entranced me with a soft-shoe dance, the first I'd ever seen—or heard, that rhythmic slip slip slip. He had that marvelous creation, the mind of a Yankee tinker. He understood machines and could fix anything.

Summer also was the time to repair and build bridges and clean culverts and ditches. Cleaning culverts was all shovel work. Ditches also were shovel work unless the road grader could straddle a ditch and tilt its blade sharply enough to gouge it out.

Most of the town's bridges were plank—large diameter metal culverts not having arrived on the scene. The plank bridges were simple affairs, with planks laid across wood or steel stringers. Entries concerning bridges regularly appeared in the road commissioner's report in the Town Report. In 1934, several entries read: H. Wilbur Reynolds, 1000 ft. 3 in. bridge plank at .02 per ft., $20.00; August Reusel, 5 bridge stringers, $5.00. The village had only one concrete bridge that I can remember—across Blood Brook by Comery Cook's garage.

The third season, dust, seemed a biblical plague, visited alike on the virtuous and sinners. No doubt I cursed it, but I also liked the scent, a part of the season's rich sachet. If you were driving, you kept well behind the car in front. A clean car on Saturday night spoke of a date for a dance.

Keeping dust down by spraying roads with water and oil was tried with limited success. Calcium chloride did work, dampening the dust with the moisture it attracted from the air. A truck would go by our place with a man standing in the dump body swinging shovelfuls of crystals that made white crescents across the road. I don't recall this being done to all roads in town. Roads through the woods didn't need attention. They stayed a damp brown. Entering from the white light of noon was like catching the breeze from an open refrigerator door.

Mudtime, the second season, tried men's souls and axles. It also fulfilled the Vermonter's need for adversity. Things going well filled him with foreboding. The gloomy prediction during a spell of good weather would be, "We'll pay for it!" The spring thaw would begin toward the end of February, if the winter had been short, or later in March. Snow on the fields looked rotten. Water covered the ice on ponds. Ditches filled and ice-filled culverts overflowed. The top few inches of road surfaces turned gooey, and the underlying, unthawed ice made for slick driving.

The tire and towing chains and shovels carried during winter were kept handy. Putting on chains in winter froze fingers, but it was a clean job; not so if your wheels were mired in mud. As the thaw progressed, the mud deepened. Spring work was heavy work. The town dumped sand and gravel on the softest spots in the roads to dry them out and used the road grader to fill in ruts and holes. Farmers helped smooth the roads near their places. They would construct a V from heavy timbers and spike a plank across to hold the V's legs apart. Horses pulled the contraption to smooth the ruts, the farmer standing on the crosspiece leaning back on the reins for steadiness. Will Bond worked on the road between our house and his, using a large diameter, wide-tread, iron wagon tire with a plank bolted across it, riding it the same way. The road commissioner had plenty of help during mudtime: farmers, unable to get onto their fields to start spring work, were free for other jobs. Those with trucks and some with teams hired out to the town. These expenses, too, were recorded in detail and published in the Town Report. Items like W.O. Blood, 2 days turning water and labor at 2.25, $5.50; Arthur Hazen, 3 days team work at 4.50, $13.50; Ernest Fitzgerald, 4 days labor at $4.00. The Town Report for the year ending January 31, 1934 devoted 25 of the report's 73 pages to roads. This was an account of the town's annual biography. Citizens could see where their tax money was going.

As roads thawed, sap rose. Mudtime also was sugaring time. Sap buckets gleamed on maple trunks. Smoke curled from sugaring houses where the evaporators thickened thin maple blood into syrup. The evaporators were slanted and had corrugated surfaces. Sap coming in at the top and trickling down the hot, hot metal had boiled into syrup by the bottom. The typical ratio was thirty quarts of sap to one quart of syrup—more if the sap that year was less sweet.

At our house, we had a small sugaring operation, making a few gallons a year. My father built a brick arch down near the brook and tapped the couple dozen maples nearest our house, one spigot and sap pail per tree—except for big trees, which had two. At the end of the run, he and the hired man used dowels to plug the holes left by the withdrawn spigots. He and the hired man—and we kids when we were big enough—carried the sap in fat five gallon buckets hung from yokes father had made for the purpose. He boiled the sap in three flat pans, bailing the liquid toward the pan nearest the chimney as it thickened. When this was thought ready, he poured it into a big pot and my mother finished it in the kitchen, using a specific-gravity gadget to determine the correct thickness.

We youngsters and teenagers knew about roads in all three seasons, walking and on bicycles. Winter provided the most excitement—depending on the gift of plentiful snow.

Officialdom having prepared the way by plowing the thick snow, and with the surface packed by the tires of a few cars, the neighborhood would gather at the hill by our house, "our hill." It was the longest and steepest readily available. Flexible Flyers were readied, their slats freshly varnished, and their runners polished bright with sandpaper and steel wool. If we were short of sleds, we'd lie down on each other, stacked double, sometimes triple, the bottom guy, nose inches from the snow, steering while groaning under the weight. We rarely sat on the sled and steered with our feet, thinking we had less control that way and were more likely to break a leg. If rain and a freeze followed the snow, the road would challenge us with ice, a genuinely risky proposition. Returning from the village, my mother's car once achieved a 360 degree skid on our hill.

Then there was Vernon Hall's travis: a heavy plank about ten feet long and twenty inches wide with iron-shod wooden sleds front and rear. The hind one was fixed; the front sled turned on a thick bolt. Vernon, older and stronger than we were, steered with ropes like reins fed through holes in the tips of the front sled. He braced his feet against a cross bar. Five or six of us would pile on, each one holding the outstretched legs of the one behind. The first passenger would tuck his feet under Vernon's bent knees. We'd start above our house by Will Bond's, yelling into the first curve. Past our house we'd accelerate by Fred Ammel's farm and head into a slight left bend to cross the upward-slanting, Blood Brook bridge, coasting to a stop. The bridge had steel girders, planks, wood railings, and crossed a gorge forty feet deep. Somebody or something must look after fools and sledders: on our descents we never met a car or brushed the bridge railings. My father once suggested that we post a lookout with a clear view down to the bridge. I doubt we heeded this good advice. Pulses thumping and eyes streaming, we'd critique the ride before hauling the beast up to Will's for another. I can't recall girls sliding with us.

We had clear sledding until the town sanded the hill, having taken care of the back roads first. Salt and calcium chloride weren't put on roads then to melt snow and ice, thus making roads sloppy and polluting streams. Then we'd hang up our sleds, return to skiing, or go skating on the rink the firemen had frozen on the common. If it had rained on the snow and then frozen to a crust hard enough to walk on, we might take toboggans to a long-sloping hill-field for truly wild rides. A toboggan on crust is an unguided missile. Lee McVetty, a Black Watch soldier during the first war, once was enticed to join us. Asked about it later, he said, "Mr. Jesus wahnt we travelin'!"

Age sixteen brought me a driver's license. Soon thereafter, I acquired a red 1928 LaSalle convertible roadster. It was a great snow car with its twenty-inch wheels and large engine. With a couple hundred pounds of sand in the back, it could go pretty near anywhere. Good snow cars were a special breed, the pride of their owners, the envy of others. Like a good horse—a prize possession, part quarter horse and part Percheron—they were to be congratulated on their performance and slapped affectionately on the rear fender. Getting from and to our house was my first challenge. I had to be cautious enough not to skid at the Blood Brook bridge and calculate when to gun it on the other side to make the waiting hill.

Norwich Hill, as it was universally called, presented another test. I had to go down and up its hundred yards to the Connecticut River every day to get to class at Dartmouth and home again. The road from Hanover crossed the Connecticut river, went past Lewiston's few houses and the grain store to the dry bridge over the Boston and Maine railway tracks. There it curved sharply right and left under a high bank, the grade steepening till it tipped onto Norwich Plain. The first turn called for discretion in any weather. To hold the turn with snow on the road you had to slow way down, losing much of the momentum needed to make the hill, or keep up speed, which risked skidding into a down-coming car, already hanging on by the skin of its treads to make it onto the bridge. Once into the curve many a driver stepped on the gas hoping to make the hill. If you spun your wheels, you were likely to slide sideways into the snow bank. Backing down for another try, might produce the same result and prevent the next driver from getting as far as you had. Result: a file of helpless machines and hapless drivers, sure to be very late for supper.

The Red Terror, self confident, would have none of this. After slowing it appropriately for the curve right, I would swing it left, just avoiding the incapacitated cars. Snorting—for it had no muffler—Terror and I would head up the hill. I sat on the high seat, feeling through the big steering wheel for an incipient skid and with a sharp ear on engine sound so that I could shift down—double-clutching like a truck—without losing traction. William Ernest Henley-like, I was the master of the elements, the captain of the hill. Later, at Merrill's store, should anyone ask, "How's the Hill?," I could answer offhandedly, "My buggy made it OK."

For the faint of heart there was a route from the river bridge out River Road to Joe Pilver's house, where you could join Route 5 and drive up a shallow hill into the village from the north. Joe, a former bootlegger and an abusive man, caused great excitement when he came to school to find his fleeing daughter. She was hiding in the girls' toilet, and Miz Cross wouldn't let him look for her there.

Sad to report, Norwich Hill is gone, the victim of an interchange leading onto Interstate 91 passing nearby. The two curves have been obliterated and the road leads up an anaemic slope from the dry bridge to Norwich Plain. A modern generation, lacking a sense of adventure and the classic skills of snow driving, doesn't know the fun it is missing, making challenging hills, cruising smoothly along pure white roads on silent tires.

The bridge crossing the river, named after Dartmouth's famous canoer-explorer John Ledyard, had a history of contention. Built in 1797 at the spot where two early settler families had crossed from New Hampshire in a canoe, with a cow swimming behind, the Hanover citizens said it had to be a toll bridge. They won over the dissent of Norwichers, who said in that case they would make do with the rope ferry half mile upstream. In 1859, Norwich and Hanover cooperated to build—for about $6,500—the covered Ledyard Free Bridge. I admired it as a boy for its two-foot thick arcs of laminated wood, set on piers in the river, that carried the floor, walls, and roof. Like so many graceful things, this was replaced by concrete and steel. The towns of Norwich and Hanover dedicated this bridge barely in time to withstand the 1938 flood, the towns having dumped tons of sand on the upstream edge to prevent the flood from tipping it over. An even fancier, and wider, bridge is there now to speed the escape from Hanover into Norwich.

Norwich neither vanquished nor was vanquished by the problems of roads and weather. The three seasons were occupations in themselves, to be sworn at or enjoyed—in any case, worked in.

Times have changed, but there never was a road that didn't need tending. I expect that townspeople still complain about *their* road. The old chores persist, and the road commissioner's job never will be easy. I hope newcomers will mourn what they've missed.

CHAPTER SEVEN

TRACY HALL

Tracy Hall was not an eligible young lady. "She" was big and brick.

Officially named Tracy Memorial Hall, dedicated in 1939, the building occupied the corner property bequeathed to the town for the purpose by James B. Tracy, along with his estate of $8,000 and a house worth $3,000. A bronze plaque at the entrance of the great hall describes this generosity, along with a large photo of Tracy in his Civil War uniform—Company K of the 16th Vermont Regiment.

Town meeting had voted to build a hall for future meetings; to house town offices and the post office; to provide a venue for suppers by the Grange, the Fish and Game Club, and suchlike gourmet occasions; and to provide a large space for basketball, square dances, and the audiences for school plays. Until 1940, meetings had been held in Union Hall, the floor above Merrill's General Store, which had become too small for the town's expanding population.

Community suppers were held in the hall's basement, equipped with a sizable kitchen and room for many trestle tables. Grange suppers were home cooking: meat, mashed potatoes and gravy, chicken pot pies, fresh vegetables, cakes and pies galore, and butter and varieties of homemade bread. Drink was tea and gallons of coffee. Most everybody knew most everybody else. Energetic talk mingled with hearty laughter. Today's heads of state might be converted to peaceableness by the experience. Game suppers put on by the Fish and Game Club followed the pattern, except that the protein came in the form of venison, sometimes bear steak, partridge, depending upon availability, and trout and bass for fish. I think these must have been bought, too large an amount to have been landed locally. Ross McKenny, former head of the Maine Guides' Association and outdoor advisor to the Dartmouth Outing Club, was a popular after-dinner speaker with tall tales and sound advice about hunting and fishing. Ross could make a canoe sit up and talk, and he could chop a log so smoothly it appeared to have been sawn. He had a genius for imparting his skills and his woods-wisdom to lovers of nature, young and older.

Friday nights, especially in winter when cold and dark evenings drove villagers and visitors indoors, young and old danced square dances and polkas in the main hall. The caller and the fiddlers were town men. Standing quietly in a corner, Fred Fitzgerald, the town constable, assured decorum. A glance from the palest blue eyes of this slender man instantly would cool off the rambunctious. He needed no uniform or weapon. Informality reigned. Unattached women and girls stood along the right-hand wall, men and boys on the left. Occasionally a girl would cross the empty floor for a partner, under the speculative gaze of the assembly. Usually boys made the trip. After that dance, either partner could relinquish the other or retain possession. The caller might announce a round dance, a mixer, like a Paul Jones. All could join in. You joined a circle of dancers holding hands, female alternating with male. The caller would command males to dance with the female so many to the right or left. One night I found myself paired with a sizable woman. When the caller hollered swing your partner, I tried, and so did she. My feet left the floor.

Merry makers engaged in these above-ground activities were unaware of the epic skirmishes that had taken place below their feet while the hall was being built. The wood forms for the hall's concrete foundations had been wide enough for young shoulders and tall enough for sneaking. With machine pistol at the ready, we inched along, holding our breath the better to locate the enemy from his breathing, peering slyly into cross trenches for a snap shot. We gained practical experience in trench warfare and armed close combat, tasting the joys of the hunt. If today's US commandos and strike forces had been trained in James Tracy's trenches, as we were, the nation's wars would have been won more readily. Like the weapons to be found along the road to Khyber, ours were country made with indigenous materials. They were rubber guns.

To manufacture a rubber gun, start with a piece of planed wood maybe 1 inch thick by 2 inches high by 20 inches long. Take a spring clothespin and screw one leg to one end of the wood "barrel" so that its pinching jaws are barely above the 2-inch height. Nail a nail where the trigger would be if this were an ordinary pistol. Now to ammunition. From a friendly garageman get a discarded car tire inner tube (remember them?) and cut it into rings an inch wide. Place a loop of the ring over the "muzzle" of the weapon and stretch the ring so that you can double the other end into a small loop and put this between the clothespin jaws. You fire by squeezing the clothespin open with the heel of your hand, possible with the purchase provided by the nail-"trigger" you have placed a few inches forward of the clothespin. The loosed rubber ring, accurate to about eight feet if you have stretched the rubber tight enough, stuns your enemy for at least a nanosecond. You can steady your aim with another nail a couple inches short of the muzzle. If your defensive or offensive situation calls for a longer-range weapon, make a carbine with a longer barrel. (Blueprints and instructions upon demand.)

The ladies do-si-do-ing in the great room of the finished hall were untutored about the heroism that had been exhibited beneath them. Nor were they aware how this experience had prepared me and my fellow veterans for service in the Vermont State Guard, whose Norwich company set up headquarters in Tracy Hall in 1941. This was a welcome but hardly a startling development, for Vermont did not intend to be run over by Germans, or Japanese, and we'd long been leery of them folks over to New Hampshire. Clearly prescient, in April 1941 the state legislature established a militia and authorized the formation of 15 State Guard companies. My father was chosen captain and served until February 1942, when he took the train to Boston to resume the navy commission he had resigned in 1920.

Oldsters and youngsters (I was fourteen), farmers, doctors, professors, and a scattering of World War I veterans joined. The professors discovered that the farmers and townspeople were as smart as they, and the latter discovered that all-right guys walked in those gowns. The existing town versus gown sentiment disappeared. Montpelier provided uniforms, helmets, packsacks, and Lee Enfield rifles. Properly rigged out, we met and drilled in the great room of Tracy Hall. We studied the *Articles of War*, learned the *Manual of Arms*, map reading, close order drill, deploying in formation, mounting guard, care of weapons—including taking our rifles and tommy guns to pieces and reassembling them in the dark. I was fascinated to learn how to use a topographical map to plot enfilading fire in hilly terrain.

Close order drill was complicated and not entirely logical. Did you turn toward the right or the left when ordered "about face?" Why make a square turn when going right or left instead of simply walking around the corner?

How to bear your rifle at port and shoulder arms? What was present arms? When hunting and not at the ready, Vermonters carry their rifles at "trail," that is, in one hand parallel to the ground, or butt in hand and barrel sloped over the shoulder. Carried sloped during an about face, your rifle knocks the head off the man in front of you, and you may lose your head to the man behind. Nearly every man acquired bruises. Paul Metcalf had special trouble. His sloped rifle inflicted many whacks, and he received his share.

The Metcalf farm covered much of Metcalf Hill. Three siblings lived in the old house: Fred was slender and slightly stooped, had balding white hair and a dental plate that whistled. He played the organ in the Congregational and Episcopal churches just across the common from each another. Abbie was a reticently charming, string bean of a lady, and a helpful librarian at Dartmouth; Paul stayed on the hill and worked the farm. To the surprise of many, he showed up at the first drill and became a regular. He walked as though he carried a pail of milk in each hand. We discovered a twinkle behind his eyes, the more fetching because it glimmered so seldom. He listened but didn't talk. Words rarely escaped his drooping mustache. Beside him, a mute was verbose.

If Paul broke his legendary silence, we listened. The company was coming back to town from a regimental bivouac near Burlington in a tired bus with our equipment stashed in racks above our heads. We hit a grade crossing and the jolt buried us under an avalanche of rifles, helmets, and packs. With profanity exhausted and order restored, Paul allowed that put him in mind of a story. A star in the East would not have commanded greater attention. "These two fellers was drivin' along hell-to-clatter," he began, "when they come to a grade crossin' and took off. They went a ways, and the passenger feller got some nervous lookin' so far daown. The driver he wahnt paying no mind, just drivin' along. The other feller looks down again and says to the driver, 'you suppose the good lawd's with us?' The driver he leans over the side. 'Well,' he says, 'if he is, he's travelin' some.'"

Once during my enlistment, a colonel from Montpelier came to Norwich to inspect our company. Assembled in Tracy Hall, our officers told us that we were to demonstrate mounting guard. The officers had taught us that a sentry's greatest sin was to let go of his rifle. They warned that the colonel would try to trick us. The first two sentries did well. The inspector came to Bub Pierce, a youngish farmer apparently eight feet tall and three feet wide, mild and deliberate. Bub ordered the colonel to halt and give the password. Receiving it, Bub ordered the colonel to advance. Then the sweet talking started.

"How are you, son? You like being in the guard? You like your officers?" Bub answered good to the first and yes to the others. "I suppose they teach you to keep your rifle clean."

"Yes, sir."

"Let's have a look." Bub extended the rifle from his position at port arms. Just as the colonel got a grip on it, Bub realized his peril. He pulled the weapon up and back, and the colonel went with it—chinning himself, or being chinned, toes reaching for the floor. A diplomatic crisis, but the standoff ended amicably. Score: Norwich 1, Montpelier 0.

————

CHAPTER EIGHT

HAYING

Two decisions precede haying: one based on judgment, one on divination. The judgment call is whether the grass is ripe, ready for cutting, as tall as it is going to grow while keeping its nutritional value. Fred Ammel had been eyeing the field for days, occasionally tasting a few spears. Divination, truth to tell, is guesswork: will it rain during the next three of four days? If not, the next day would be for mowing. Days two and three would be for drying (the sun needed to be hot), and day four was for more drying and getting the crop into the barn.

A wrong calculation here and rain could ruin the crop. If the mowing was left in the field to redry, hay lost value, and before bringing it in, Fred had to get the damp out of it, which he did by fluffing it with a pitchfork—a very long job—or by using a tedder, a machine with multiple heels, that kicked up bunches of the mowing. Damp hay actually could be dangerous, combusting spontaneously and setting the barn on fire.

With all elements apparently favorable for action, the mower and the rake came out of the wagon shed and the hay wagon (rack or rick) out of the hay barn, to be checked and greased. Fred called the greasegun the most important tool on the farm. The mower, for those unacquainted with one, was drawn by two horses, with an iron, butt-molded seat for the driver—with holes in it to drain any rain. Beside the driver, a tall lever engaged the cutter bar. This projected from the right hand side of the mower, and its blades slid back and forth in its housing similar to an urbanite's hedge clipper.

In the fields, all was an adventure. I loved the "slip slip" sound of the cutter, the neat, flat rows where it had mown, the perfume in my nose, which had been caught in the line in the old song, *On the Banks of the Wabash Far Away:* "From the fields there comes the breath of new-mown hay." When I reached the age of twelve or so I was allowed to drive the one-horse rake, its seat well above its long curved tines rolling the hay behind me into thick, eight-foot-long sausages called windrows. Kicking a pedal made the tines rise to leave the windrow to be folded into tumbles.

One time Fred cut it pretty close. The thunder was grumbling distantly, and building the load he muttered, "Guess we'll make it." The sun brightened the stubble, and the remaining tumbles (called haycocks by some) cast pale shadows while waiting to be forked up onto the wagon. A small breeze carried the damp of impending rain. The thunder sounded a bit louder, and gray clouds appeared over the hill at the end of the meadow.

Better get a move on, the crew thought, and they speeded up without hurrying. The fringes of the gray clouds began to cover the sun as black clouds followed the gray over the hill. Fred turned the horses closer to those half-dozen remaining tumbles. With these aboard, he headed for the barn. A few drops of rain fell as he reached it. "Jest in time," he said, driving in.

The men forked the load into the bays on each side of the rick (wagon) and stood wiping their faces. Through the tall doors, framed by the barn's blackness, they watched the sheets of rain sweep the field. The horses fidgeted as lightening cracked and thunder rumbled. There's no place better to watch a thunderstorm than through a hay-barn door.

Robert Frost wrote a poem entitled "The Code" about men and haying. He painted the scene using his skill with the rhythms of speech. His scene was familiar to me.

My father, sister, I, and others used to help Fred Ammel hay. We would fork the tumbles up to Fred building the load on the flatbed rick. He'd lay tumbles along its edges as far out as they could go without falling off, and then place a line of tumbles down the center to bind the load together. Up and up till the load was tall and tight. Fred had the knack. I wasn't much help when the load grew tall. Even my pitch fork wouldn't reach. I was free to mop my face and wipe the hayseed from under my belt.

The load built, Fred would drive to the barn, up an earth ramp and stop when the load was just inside—and the team deep inside—the tall double doors. This put him about two and a half stories up in about a four-story barn. Below the wagon on each side were deep bays, sometimes filled first, as just described, and below them the cow stanchions. Fred forked the hay into the bays while the horses munched and snuffled. I would be sent into a bay to spread the hay and tread it down. One day the thick dust so parched my mouth that to generate some saliva, I asked one of the men for a chaw; he tossed me his cut plug. I gnawed off a chunk. I got the spit all right, along with a queasy stomach and a twirling head. I climbed out of the bay and went outside to lie on the grass. Moral: Don't bite off what you're not man enough to chew.

When the bays were full, subsequent loads went onto the mow, just over the team's heads. Fred would stomp a U-shaped hay fork with thirty-inch prongs into the load. Hitched to a ring at the top of the fork, a rope ascended to a pulley on the track running into the barn. The rope's other end descended to the rake horse, doing double duty. When the horse pulled on the rope the bundle of hay rose to the track, hit a switch and then ran along the track until over the mow. Fred then pulled a trip line that retracted the fingers on the prongs, thus allowing the hay to drop. Hay unloaded, we drank ginger beer, and headed for the field. Making a load, bringing and storing it, took a little more than an hour.

The scene set, we return to Frost. In "The Code," he describes three men haying, two farmers, one building the load, the other pitching up, and a "town-bred farmer." The ground man marches off, mad, and the town-bred man asks why. The remaining farmer explains, you made a remark about speeding up the work and James took offense. He then offers a piece of advice:

> The hand that knows his business won't be told
> To do work better or faster...

Then he tells a story about when he was haying and paired off with a bully boss. He had built the load and driven into the barn, ready to unload into the bay:

> "...The old fool seizes his fork in both hands,
> And looking bewhiskered out of the pit,
> Shouts like an army captain, 'Let her come!'
> Thinks I, D'ye mean it? 'What was that you said?'
> I asked out loud so's there'd be no mistake.
> 'Did you say, Let her come?' 'Yes. Let her come.'
> He said it over, but he said it softer."

(What a wonderful line.)

Mad himself by now, the story teller tells the town farmer that he finds the key tumble in the load and "dumped the rackful on him in ten lots." The boss survived. The town farmer asks, "Did he discharge you?"

"Did he discharge me? No! He knew I did just right."

CHAPTER NINE

ICE CREAM

I think it safe to assume that when Longfellow wrote the line "the thoughts of youth are long long thoughts" he wasn't thinking about milkshakes. Had he gone to Gill's Store he would have been served a real *choclet* milkshake, about which we youngsters had longing thoughts. The perfect drink, Longfellow could have drunk it and savored the bits of ice cream; none of this pallid soup that these days masquerades as milkshakes in eateries along freeways. Older, quiet, gentle Rob Olds would drop a big scoop of choclet ice cream into the metal container and follow this with a long squirt of choclet syrup from among the array of snouts. Then Rob would grope for a milk bottle under the counter, add a generous portion, and blend the ingredients with a rod whirled by the green-topped electric motor. The cost, a quarter.

A black-and-white milkshake was choclet sauce with vanilla ice cream. Like a cowboy in a saloon, leaving Longfellow behind, we'd swagger up to the bar and say, "a blackanwhite." But we said "please, Mr. Olds," or we'd be out on our ear. We could get a Coke, also hand made—with the thick, secret-formula syrup plungered from another snout and seltzer-water added from yet another. A lemon Coke—with a dash of lemon syrup—was a special adventure. No oasis could have meant more to a desert traveler than Gills to us. The store sat in the V where Mechanic Street went left toward Old Howard's blacksmith shop and Main Street went straight ahead. Gossip had it that Old Howard clinched horse shoes just loose enough to get added business as owners and horses had to return for a fitting sooner than expected.

Wood steps stretched the width of the store, worn whitish from feet treading to the double doors between big windows. I can't remember what these displayed, but directly at the back as you entered was the soda fountain. For a short time before the uncommonly good and the rigidly righteous took notice, the store had a pinball machine that paid off. A nickel got you three balls, and if they fell into the right holes, the machine paid. You opened a little door in the front and swept out nickels proportionate to your score. Jiggling the machine to make the balls go into the right holes was an art. For if shaken too hard, the machine would retaliate: the display would light up, "Tilt," and you'd lost your nickel.

The shelves on the right and left walls of the store held medicines and whatever sundries were. A brown metal container fastened to one wall contained an unknown. Maybe it was two feet wide and three feet high. On its sliding door in gold letters were listed the ailments the contents were to cure. The last of those was "Feminine

Complaints." I've heard a number of feminine complaints in my time—several with my name attached. But those behind the gold letters remain a mystery.

Having drunk my Coke (lemon?) or milkshake or made a purchase, I left down the steps. I was not to tarry on them. Father had warned me against becoming a drug-store cowboy.

Norwich, when I was ten or twelve, had a band and a bandstand, which is still standing, on the common. Concerts on summer Saturday evenings began about dusk after cars parking on the common had nearly encircled it. Honking horns and flicked headlights indicated approval, drowning out the applause of those who had come on foot. I think I enjoyed the music, especially the flute player. A Vermont individualist, he not only marched to a different drummer, he fluted to a different conductor. His arpeggios soared though the maple leaves as the band played on.

I remember, too, the profits from those evenings. Richard Putnam had opened a branch of his father's Hanover drug-store in the village. Dick conceived the idea of selling ice cream to concert goers and looked to us kids as vendors. He filled cardboard boxes with chocolate and vanilla cones, held upright in holes in a cardboard insert. We'd dash down the street and offer our wares to standees and through car windows. Price a nickel, for which we got a penny commission. Sold out, we'd dash back for another load—at a greater speed on drippy nights. If, after the market crashed, one cone didn't sell, Dick didn't begrudge us the treat.

It was an honest profit, earned by vigorous promotion and being fast on our feet. My 35-cent take—on a good night—was pure, unsullied by corporate welfare. I'd like to say that with it I built the foundation of my fortune. It was not to be. I lavished it on wine and women, reducing myself to my current impecunious state.

Town Meeting in 1939 appropriated $100 to the band to support the concerts.

CHAPTER TEN

AN UNPRECEDENTED ACCOLADE

The first Tuesday after the first Monday in March, 1973, is not mentioned as the date of a notable event in any compendium of which I am aware. Yet on that day, when Vermonters hold their town meetings, the citizens of Norwich, typically not given to accord on education matters, bestowed an unprecedented accolade. They voted unanimously to change the name of the Norwich Public School to the Marion W. Cross School. This was to be displayed in white letters on a black band arched over the double front doors, as its predecessor had been.

Fourteen years after this event, I spent a week listening to Marion Cross's memories of a life teaching children— she never called them kids—from grades one through eight. She spoke about the craft of teaching from her first job, in 1925; of her love of English as a language and teaching it as a subject; of her methods for keeping order in the classroom; and of the family life that had molded her.

I had nurtured the wish to write about Miz Cross since I had left her school and the village. In the summer of 1987 I had my chance. Then, I called upon her and said I'd like to write about her. Would she like to talk with me,

and let me record her memories? After brief thought she
agreed, and the next day I returned with tape recorder for
sessions that lasted a week. She was living in a light, airy,
small apartment in a complex built for elderly individuals
behind the Norwich Public Library—a small brick box on
Main Street built in 1902, open on Saturday afternoons.
The town meeting annually appropriated $200 to the
library to assure the books "would be free for all." On one
wall of her living room hung a picture of a maple tree in
fall plumage on the edge of the school grounds. She had
helped plant that tree, she said, that is, "I watched with
my eighth graders while the men planted it. I never let the
children climb that one." On another wall hung a painting with Mt. Mansfield in the background, "the view from
my bedroom in the old home place in Johnson," she said.
"When I look at that, Norwich, happy as I've been here,
isn't the same."

We sat at the kitchen table. Soft airs came in the open
windows, accompanied now and then by the caretaker's
lawnmower's drone—very present on my tape recorder.
Each morning Miz Cross made us coffee and there was a
plate with either sandwiches or doughnuts. As a doughnut
freak, I ate more than my share. Her ginger cat made occasional appearances, rubbed shins, approached laps, and had
to be shooed off the table. The atmosphere was relaxed:
time had mellowed any teacher-pupil distinction.

She seemed to me to have changed little over the
years. She was a model for the typically inaccurate remark,

"You haven't changed a bit." Older looking, yes, but little changed I thought from 1940 when I joined her seventh grade. Her hair had grayed slightly, but she was as slender as ever. She carried her head at a slight rightward tilt, and her lips had the same inclination—expressing wry humor and skepticism with warmth. Gone was the expression she seemed to direct at me during my school days: I-know-more-about-you-than-you-think-I-do. Which, in all likelihood, she did. She still lit up when she laughed, which was readily. Only rarely had townspeople or pupils thought her stern.

She had a position in the township and village of Norwich that no single word describes—at least one I know. "Prominent" conveys a grandiose bearing and habiliments beyond a mackinaw in winter and a summer cotton dress and, in all weathers, sensible shoes. Unlike Richard Cory, she didn't glitter when she walked. "Pillar" of the community connotes thick and tall, which she was not. "Personality" comes the closest, perhaps, if a "personality" may be unassuming—a known, liked, and much respected quantity. "Presence" may come next. If modesty is pride concealed, she had neither. She was Miz Cross, teacher. "Miz," designated neither Miss nor Mrs, for it applied to either condition and was used for all females except young girls.

Behind her friendly exterior Marion Cross had stored four decades of teaching experience, well considered into a sharp-witted humanism. Individuals who went to her school, their parents, and the teachers who taught with her and under her as principal, speak of her administrative ability, her sympathetic openness while guiding their teaching, and her mentoring of teachers newly come to the school. "Because she had these qualities and expected excellence both in the classroom and out of school," remembered a teacher, "she made a big difference to the school. Part of her success came from her insistence that parents are a teacher's business; teachers should teach parents about teaching."

Her methods were considered ahead of their time; yet she continued to absorb fresh ideas and techniques. She thought a teacher's experience more effective for pupils' learning than having studied the philosophy of education in teachers' college or university. To monitor each pupil's progress, teachers wrote their own tests—the exceptions being for math and science, where company-designed tests were used—and discussed results with the pupil. Pupils needing extra help were to be brought along at their own speed. A child should not be kept back after the fifth grade, Miz Cross believed, and remedial help should come at the beginning of the next grade. She used brighter pupils to help slower ones, challenging both. "Children are eager to learn things they know are for older children," Miz Cross believed. She believed that exercise during school hours released energy and tension and improved performance back in the classroom—a new idea today, appearing in education publications—even to calisthenics during class.

In my day we had 15 minute recesses, at 10:30 in the morning and 2:30 in the afternoon.

Perhaps most unusual of Miz Cross's educational policies, in comparison to those of today, was her emphasis on reading and writing English. "We all knew these were always on her mind," a teacher recalled. Their importance is borne out by the poor quality of comprehension and writing in high schools and colleges today. Miz Cross was firm on order in classrooms, not discipline, a word she disliked. She maintained order by radiating her expectation that she should receive deference, that her command was certain. Also, she never dressed down a pupil in front of others, and she kept a step ahead of mischief makers. Although polite, "her look of disapproval would straighten out a child," a former teacher said. She expected that pupils leaving her eighth grade would have acquired character and manners: "Education is more than book learning." I became aware of these characteristics when I had Miz Cross for the seventh and eighth grades in 1940 and 1941, and because she had been a presence in her pupils' lives since they entered first grade, which I did in 1933. She had been teaching in the Norwich school since 1931, the fifth and sixth grades to start with and thereafter the seventh and eighth.

An aside: Miz. Cross may have learned a lot about me as I went through the grades and into her room, and she may have surmised more. But not about my dark secret: I had had a love affair. In those days a photographer visited annually to take pictures of pupils for sale to them and to gullible parents. Mine, either proud or tolerant, bought several of these two-inch square Avedons. No surprise. But when I bought one of Bertha Cook, sneaky giggles greeted me. They were nothing compared to the razzing I got at home from mother, father, brother and sister. Insensitive persons, they were unable to acknowledge profound emotion. Deeply embarrassed, indeed wounded, by such scorn, I had to rid myself of the object.

At the end of one of our sheds at home, by the gate from the paddock into the pasture, stood a tall white pine with its roots perhaps nourished by the septic tank my father had dug under it. I climbed to the very top, bearing Bertha tenderly. Providentially, there was a robin's nest there, and Bertha came to snuggle among the three pale blue eggs.

Aside within an aside: I had two other new experiences in first grade. I was inspected for head lice, along with classmates, by a school nurse imported for the purpose. At Christmas we all were given a pair of knitted woolen mittens paid for by a trust established by an unnamed elderly lady. Seasoned by the three experiences, I graduated to second grade.

I invited Miz Cross to start reminiscing where she would. She began at her beginnings—in Johnson, Vermont. She seemed to get as much pleasure from remembering as I did from listening.

Her great, great grandparents had bought the land and the house where she was born in 1907, she said. Her grandfather had been born there. So had her father. She remembered that it was a lovely house to grow up in, wood and white. From her second floor windows she could look west to Mt. Mansfield and from the other side of the room down into the village. At the rear of the house her grand-father had added an ell built with bricks from his own kiln. He had fought in the Civil War and she remembered him, although he lived for only a few years after she was born. To commemorate grandfather's service her father took the family to church the Sunday before Memorial Day and after church to the cemetery. She thought her father would have liked to have been in a war. Grandmother lived on, crippled from causes Miz Cross couldn't recall, and her family had a woman to help with her.

"Father owned and ran the farm until his very last years," Miz Cross said. "He milked the Holstein cows that he loved, keeping them in a big barn with his horses. These were western horses, which he wanted to go up our hills. He was good natured except when those cows wouldn't come in the morning for milking. We had a big potato patch behind the barn. For quite a few years Dad was the town's road commissioner. That's an awful hard job, but he was never afraid of work. And he never minded people finding fault. Wintertimes he plowed the roads with his horses. It always seemed to be freezing cold. He knew everyone in town, and everyone knew him. Speaks well of him that he still had so many friends after that job," she said, chuckling.

We paused for doughnuts. "Pretty good, aren't they," she said. "My daughter-in-law, Neil's wife, makes them. Have a little more coffee?"

Between bites, Miz Cross continued. "Dad had a real Irish sense of humor and always had a yarn. He could entertain for hours. Not always much truth in what he said; he'd add a bit but it made a good story. Neighbors would come in, and I could hear them laughing, having the best time. Dad was humorous, and I mean humorous, no stupid stuff. He could mimic anybody. Mother loved his stories, never a naughty one. He'd read aloud, too. My mother's brother was a veterinarian from down somewhere in Massachusetts. He'd come up and stay a few nights. 'Perley, read us something,' he'd say. That was thrilling for me. My father's name was Dexter Perley Whiting, everybody called him Perley. He'd been a Republican all his life. In 1932 he went to one of the other selectmen and explained he was going to become a Democrat: 'I'm going to vote for Roosevelt. Should I resign from the board? Some people think I should not be on it if I'm going to vote Democrat.' They chatted some, and the man said go home. 'It don't matter who you vote for, you help us run this town.' Before FDR, the Whitings always were known as Republicans. Grandfather Campbell was a Democrat. He and Dad would have the darndest arguments—always pleasant, for they got on well."

Miz Cross explained that her mother's family were Campbells—Grandma Campbell was Evelyn Mary

Campbell. They had come over to Canada from Ireland
and then down to Belvidere, Vermont. They were very
strong Catholics, the strongest she ever knew. But sometime along the way, before she married her father in 1903,
her mother decided not to be a Catholic any longer. "I
thought about that a lot," Miz Cross said. The Whitings
had always been Protestants. Her mother went to the
Congregational Church a few times a year. "But believe
you me," Miz Cross added, "she saw to it that I went
almost every Sunday." I asked her if there had been anti-
Catholic prejudice in Johnson in those days. She said that
she didn't recall any, although a lot of French-Canadians
lived in Johnson. "Some called them Canucks, which
wasn't polite." When the family was visiting they walked
with mother's sisters five miles to the Catholic Church in
Hyde Park.

She loved visiting her mother's family in Belvidere. "It
was a little dump of a town, maybe not even a store. There
were three girls and three boys in the family. The youngest
girl taught school. It was a rural school, eight grades in a
room, and I couldn't wait to go with her. Later—she wasn't
old—she lost the use of her mind. Aunt Ethel, another of
mother's sisters, taught for eight years. By then she was
getting rheumatism all the time. Grampa had to carry
her to school and back every day. After that she became
a complete cripple and was in bed unless he put her in
a wheel chair. She was smart, and she used to entertain
me. I suppose I entertained her. The youngest brother also

was a cripple in a wheel chair. All those years Gramma took care of them, and she was a little body like me." She paused a while and began again. "It was a tough generation having a hard row. They were fond of each other; that must have helped. The older I grow the more I think about it: Complaining just wasn't on, no whimpering or crying or being upset about it. You took what came to you and went on the best you could. Dad used to say 'if there's a saint on earth, it's grandmother Campbell.' If I could have been as good Catholics as they were, and take what they did, I could be a Catholic."

"Summers in Belvidere I drove the hayrake. Grampa Campbell was really something. He bought and sold businesses. He bought an automobile and drove it for a year or two without a license. We'd pitch down some of those steep hills. When I went with Grampa to Belvidere, father said he used to pray that we'd get there, and if we got there that I'd get back. The town sent Grampa to the state legislature in Montpelier for a year."

Miz Cross chuckled and gently moved the cat off the table. "Kitty, you get down. Sandwiches are not for you; now don't bother him." I told her that I like cats.

Her family was a big part of her growing up, she resumed. Sometimes life was hard; it was always simple. We had good times. "Mother and Dad really liked each other," she said. "I used to wonder why they were so happy. I think it was because they were making the best out of a bad job. Inheriting a farm isn't all that some people think it is. Mother sewed for me so I'd have more than two dresses for school. All children were like that then. I liked school. English was my favorite subject—and the subject I have liked to teach the most—even English grammar, which Mother insisted on; she'd correct my mistakes." She laughed as she recalled: "Father didn't get off easy." More laughter. "He'd come back from working in the winter woods or on the roads with lumbermen and Frenchmen speaking the worst English. Mother jumped right down his neck. Sometimes he'd be talking and she'd say 'What did you say??!!' Dad never went beyond high school, but he educated himself all his life. So I learned how to talk. You could always tell if a teacher had been taught English properly by the way she spoke. In younger grades, children are eager to learn something they know is for others a little older than they are. You can crowd some English down them that way."

"I liked school so much that when I got home I played school in the kitchen. This was lucky because I had to come right home from school every day. I even walked back and forth for lunch. One day a year I had lunch at school. That was the big day of the year. I did a lot of my schoolwork at home. If other children came home with me, we all played school. We had a blackboard on the kitchen wall, and I'd pull up chairs to the kitchen table and get out books and materials. We'd work until it was time to eat. Mother would help us. She had been a rural school teacher, too. After supper I helped mother clear up.

Those iron sinks were so hard to keep clean."

"We always had plenty of books. We all read a lot, the New England poets, especially Whittier, Longfellow, William Cullen Bryant. Robert Frost hadn't come along. I always had permission to go to the town library, which was good. Mother was the librarian for a time. I could sit by the hour and tell you things that I had as a girl that a youngster doesn't have today. Mother always was ready to help us; she always had time to give. If we asked questions, we got answers. She was always writing papers, and I'd ask what are you writing about and she'd tell me and I'd ask where are you getting your material and she'd say 'it's all around me.' She wrote well, and this did a lot for me. Before becoming a teacher, Mother'd gone to Johnson normal school. For us, Mother was a teacher, a minister, and this boils down to what's right and what's wrong."

The morning after this listening, Miz Cross leaned back and stared across the room. She wondered aloud to me, "I got to thinking in bed last night, Why on earth did I go on so about my mother and father? They were just ordinary people."

After a silence, she resumed remembering. She had skipped the third grade and did the work at home with her Mother. She didn't understand why her parents did this, and she thought it a bad idea. Through her teaching she had learned that skipping or holding a child back seldom works well. Better to bring a child along at his own speed while exerting special effort to get him ready for the next grade. This almost always made a big difference in the child. Her own fourth-grade experience wasn't particularly pleasant. She thought she'd been a bit of a problem, her mother was afraid she was getting too nervous. She had had a teacher who was really cranky, and was scared of her.

That fifth grade teacher had discipline: "I'm telling you she had discipline! She told my mother that she'd go to the back of the room and look back and I'd be sitting on the floor. Imagine! Mrs. Woodward was very stern, but she could teach like nobody's business, and you really learned. I remember her more than any teacher I ever had. She taught me the most." As to practice teachers when she was in grade school, they came from Johnson Normal School and brought variety to class because they came from around the state. (Granville, Miz Cross explained, you understand that today they call normal schools teachers colleges. My school now is named Johnson State College. Johnson had a one-year course then, now it's four, as in most teachers colleges.) Practice teaching is important, she went on, but when you're in another teacher's classroom, you teach the way she wants you to. Practice teachers and substitutes were fair game for some children, especially boys, trying to put things over on them.

Miz Cross said that she had finished grade school at age thirteen, graduated from high school at sixteen, and then went right into normal school. She remembered good teachers at Johnson and learning a lot. Discipline was strict. There were good literature and reading courses. Students heard little about the philosophy of education, just how to go out and teach. They learned much about what not to do. There was more about how to present material than about the material itself. For example, they went page by page in a history book. When she was teaching, she had children reading other than text books. Fundamentals were important, which she saw every day after she left Johnson. They were taught about teaching each of the eight grades because most of them would be sent to rural schools. There were set books for teaching each grade, and those were the ones the school focused on. The hardest thing for a teacher, Miz Cross had discovered, is to keep learning ahead and how to teach different groups of children. "I've seen high school teachers since then that I thought could have used some of the training we had. I think we got more real knowledge about children and teaching than many of those today who come directly from college. This was important because when I went out to teach eight grades in rural school I had to be prepared. Even then it was difficult. A college-trained teacher would have a broader background and could be a good teacher if the college had done a good job teaching teaching. I learned from mother's sister who boarded with mother and father while she went to normal school; she then became the school's secretary. She was an especially strong person and a great favorite, wonderful to Dad."

Miz Cross looked back happily on her life growing up. There was a lot of entertainment in Johnson, she said. Visitors came by their home; there was her father telling his stories and reading aloud. Evenings they often played cards. An uncle had left the family a good piano and her mother had paid for lessons, even though times were hard. Miz Cross played the piano in normal school, and when teaching rural school in Union Village, her second job. Additionally, she played the organ in church and some Sundays sang in the choir. "Here in Norwich," she said, "I played in the Grange Hall till about five years ago. Then my hands were too stiff, I just couldn't any more."

I suspect that without being aware of doing so Miz Cross had described a principal element in her success as a teacher—one other rural teachers of the era shared: She was one with the society of her pupils and their parents. Herself from an essentially classless society, she fitted into Norwich's egalitarianism as a familiar figure, not as an import from a society strange to them. At the same time she stood out because of her personality and her talents as a teacher and as a leader. It may be that today, particularly in big, inner-city schools, the disparity among teachers and between pupils, parents, and teachers handicaps instruction and keeping order.

Growing up, too, Miz Cross recalled, there were square dances. "I always liked dancing, maybe more than I should have," she added, making a slight face. "When I first taught, in Pleasant Valley, I had good times dancing and probably should have worked harder. We didn't have movies or a theater in Johnson—and we didn't have a car, except maybe a Ford, but not for long. But we did have the opera house with a raised stage where we put on plays and musicals. Plays were very popular and father played in them beautifully. At the normal school we had school plays and programs. People took part in things. You made your own fun. Every summer there was a Chautauqua. We didn't call it that, but it was a series of lectures by people in town and by visitors—about poetry, literature, philosophy, humorous speeches, the war in Europe."

There were sports. Johnson had a baseball team and played regular games with teams from other towns. Baseball was the game of the time. Miz Cross's father had played on the team, but not after she was born. "Winters, there was sliding. The freezing cold made the snow on the roads hard, sometimes icy. A group of boys on the hill above our farm went down that long hill, with houses on each side, right into the village. Someone had money enough to have a nice travis—a top board with a fixed sled at the rear and a front sled fastened so it could be steered. Evenings, especially, they'd load up that travis with five boys and sail right down into the village. They put a lookout where this road met a big cross street, and if they got through this all right they went on through the covered bridge. It was about a mile and a half and as much fun as anyone has nowadays. When I first came down here we did some sliding—down from Pierce's." She asked me if I knew Bub

Pierce. I told her yes. He lived in that big white house on the long hill on the Goodrich Four Corners road. He married Helen Kendall, didn't he, from across the road? We sat silently, thinking about this. I remembered Bub Pierce well, a tall fellow, husky and cheerful. We were in the Vermont State Guard in 1942—he older than I.

Miz Cross admonished the cat for returning to the table, and returned to her story. She began teaching at age 18 in Pleasant Valley near Cambridge, Vermont. That was a rural school with eight grades in the room. "I didn't do very well," she recalled. She had so much to learn and probably could have put more effort into it—and spent less time than she should have at dances and so on. "It's awful to go into teaching when you're in your teens." It was a cold winter; the school board provided the wood, and the janitor kept the stove going. All in all it was a pretty good year, she thought, and she had gained experience. At the end of it she got a better offer from Union Village and moved there in 1925. (Union Village was— and is—a small village north of Norwich village near the banks of the Pompanoosuc River.)

"That was a rural school with a lot of problems, bigger than Pleasant Valley. I loved it, but some mornings I dreaded dealing with so many different dispositions. The pay was better than when I came down to Norwich after five years. It was a small community, and I was expected to be a part of everything. Being a teacher was not a six-day a week job. I went to church on Sunday, played the organ, sang in the choir, but no teaching Sunday school: I'd had enough during the week! I helped out with church suppers and such. Parents would want to see me in the evening—when I was ready to go to bed. The school is a very important place for a rural community. It's a social center, with an event almost every week. The farther out in the country the school is and the smaller the number of farms around it, the more important the school is to those people. You feel you can do more when you're in a rural school. You always feel wanted. The best part is being your own boss."

They had a PTA in Union Village. Parents were interested in the school, and she had found that this was never a nuisance. The question for the teacher was whether to wait for the parents to come in to talk or to take the initiative. She sent around a circular letter inviting parents to come in if they wished. Usually, they preferred meetings at the schoolhouse. "In a village, people either get along or are fighting no matter their educational background. While I was there they gave full support to the school."

As demanded, Miz Cross led a decorous social life. "Teachers were supposed to be models of behavior," she said. "Otherwise, there'd be trouble. Whether the teacher liked it or not, she was a public figure." She went to square dances in Union Village with the family where she boarded. Teachers weren't supposed to smoke, especially in public. (Nor was any lady, according to my mother, who smoked like a chimney in private.) No beer or wine in public. There was an old maid from Thetford on the school board who told her she shouldn't go to so many public occasions. Miz Cross laughed as she again said, "It's awful to go into teaching when you're in your teens."

When she first came to Union Village she boarded with a Mrs. Etta Barstow. Saturday afternoon of the first weekend, Miz Barstow had her and a few young people helping to clean the church. Miz Cross had school work to do and was worried that she'd not finish it. Later Miz Barstow took in an elderly lady in a wheelchair and had to take care of her. Things got tough in the middle of the year, she was lonely, and decided to move. "I'd got to know the Gould family, and they became the closest friends in my life. A big family with six children, all bright and nice. Four of them, one time or another, came to school to me. Roy Gould had had a meat cart and a good business delivering around the village. He was active in church and acted in the plays every year. I talked it over with Roy. He said 'Mary Jane'—he always called me that—'I don't think you ought to. Etta's boarded teachers over the years. She's going to talk awfully about your going. You know that woman's tone. She hasn't said anything good about you or anybody else since I've been here. If you're sure, Mary Jane, you come down to stay with us.'"

"I broke the news to Mrs. Barstow. She didn't say very much. She must have been hurt, but I never heard a word. Roy helped me move. I lived upstairs and was carrying down a lamp. At the head of the stairs I dropped it." She laughed heartily: "The chimney broke and the kerosene went over everything. Roy never let me forget that. We didn't have electricity in the school, either; on dark winter afternoons we'd light the lamps. I learned a lot from the Goulds, especially about life in a big family."

That first year in Union Village, Miz Cross had twenty-five children, five each in grades one and eight and two or three in the other grades. "I did everything except put them to bed," she said. "It was a real test of character. One family were bootleggers. Another set of parents drank pretty heavily. Several sets of parents were functionally illiterate. Yet their children pulled through. The first day, eight children came to school dirty. I cleaned them up in school and let the family know what I'd done. Other families needed moral support. I'd comment if the girls had on something specially nice. I knew them all, and some of those children must have had it pretty hard some mornings, slapped or cussed at. Mostly, people in Union Village were average; they wanted to do a lot for their children. Others didn't care."

"When parents came to visit school, they'd ask, 'How does Johnny mind? How does he take direction? Does he seem to be all right?' If you're a young teacher starting out you think, What's Johnny like?, but Johnny would turn out to be just a normal child. Some children were bright, others needed pushing. If I'd had more time, I'd have got the slower ones up there. They had a wider ability to learn, but they had to be organized. I'd use children in the upper grades to work with the lower. A girl in the French family was bright and so helpful. I'd say, 'You are my assistant teacher,' but I had to be careful not to overuse her because she had things to learn. There was more socialization in a rural school, different ages and backgrounds all together."

"Children off the farm often were more mature," Miz Cross thought. "They usually had good minds, even if they weren't especially bright. Even a child who is not especially intelligent can talk about something he likes and talk about it well. I'd try to find a pupil's special interest, something about the farm, perhaps, and I'd say, 'Wouldn't you like to tell us about it?' That was a good way to teach fundamentals like grammar. A child would come to me and ask, 'Does this sound all right?' English comes in every class—every time you speak. I stressed simple English and writing sentences. Younger children did learn from older ones. And one thing all children learn in rural school is concentration."

"On the playground the older helped the younger. Still, I had to be johnny-on-the-spot. Usually if children play together, everything is OK. If something goes wrong, correct it right then. Recess is terribly important, getting rid of all that energy. It helps children pay attention and learn back in the classroom," she said. She wondered if educators understood this sufficiently. "To get older children to help younger was why in Norwich I organized the safety patrol and crossing guards."

Miz Cross strongly believed in teaching character. That's important, she insisted, because education is more than book learning. During my time in Miz Cross's room, I never thought my character was being built. So I conclude that we pupils absorbed it—to the extent we did—from her conduct. By the time we got out of the eighth grade we were to have it "and have good manners, too," she said. A teacher must get over to the pupil what's right and decent. You must let pupils know what you expect. "I expect I was pretty blunt letting them know what I demanded," she said, "but you must be polite. Explaining why something was wrong could get you into trouble, but I must have explained. Never shame a child in front of the others. Keeping order—I don't like the word discipline, although I do use it—is necessary. When I think discipline, I think rural school. I was willing to teach when children were willing to listen—not when half were listening and half were fiddling with something. I never could tolerate noise. Discipline includes speaking English correctly. If someone did not, I'd explain."

"There are knacks to keeping order," she went on. "I had a few tricks of my own. If you catch a child the first time, that usually makes him think you see everything. If a child in my room threw a spitball, I'd be stupid to ask, 'Did you throw that spitball?' He'd say, 'No'. So I'd say 'I don't ever want you to throw a spitball in my room again.' That surprises him and he knows you mean it. When I was principal and a teacher asked me to deal with an unruly child, I would call him out of the room and take him to a private room and leave him. Not very often did this happen a second time. Or if a teacher sent a child to my room I'd put him at the back of my room, give him a book, and tell him 'I don't want to be bothered by you.' I had little trouble with discipline here in Norwich. I did have a boy from Lewiston whose father was a card. That boy would never amount to anything, but he'll have a lot of fun. I guess the mildest comeuppance I used was making a child stay after school on Friday—when we let out at 3:30 instead of 4:00—to bang the chalk out of the erasers and wash the blackboards."

"Always keep from being disagreeable," Miz Cross continued. "You can't make a child learn. If a child thinks you're unfair, then you can't do a thing with him. And you don't know what happened before school in the morning. Was he yelled at or reasoned with? I felt sorry for a child who came to school unhappy. How could I make him contented? No candy or gush around; try to win him over. I never touched a child, don't believe that gets you anywhere. When I was young in a rural school, I could give a big child a pretty good scuffle, but you're not making your way with a child when you do that. If the situation gets that bad, the parents have to be brought in. I've lined out a few teachers in my time who were harsh with a child. In those days there were always certain boys—fewer girls—whose aim it was to get the better of the teacher. A teacher has to learn that pupils must respect her. They may hate you like poison, but that wears off if they find you fair. Parents who think their child can do no wrong are a pain in the neck."

Miz Cross may have gained her own equanimity from her mother, who got really angry only once, so far as she could remember. The family had a barn cat in Johnson, "all black and big." One day he got into the house and into the pantry where mother had pans of milk setting after father had brought the pails in from the barn. Mother saw him lapping the milk and she picked up a knife and threw it. It was a long way across the kitchen and into the pantry, "but she took that cat right in the shoulder. He came rattling down through the pans, shot by us, and right through that screen door. Mother was such a gentle person; she was so ashamed. Father never let her forget it."

When the Crosses came to Norwich in 1931, there were three of them: herself, husband Harold, and new son, Neil. She and Harold had met on a Sunday. From the choir in Union Village church she had seen a very nice looking young man enter and sit in a rear pew. When service ended the man went out and she went home to the Goulds, who lived next door. "There he was," she said, laughing, "sitting at the kitchen table talking to Roy. He introduced me to Harold Cross. Harold was a carpenter and a builder. We were married in August 1928."

The Crosses' 25th anniversary year was her parents 50th anniversary. Both families were feted in Johnson at the Whiting home. According to the account in the local paper,

> Refreshments, including an anniversary
> cake, were served by Mrs. Robert McKenzie
> (who had driven up from Norwich), Mrs.

Henry Parker, Jr., Mrs. Richard Parker, and Mrs. Ronald Hutchins. Among the gifts and congratulatory messages was a poem written for the occasion by Mary Chamberlin Reek, a classmate of Mrs. Whiting at Johnson State Normal School. Out of town guests included Mr. and Mrs. Harold Cross and their son, Neil; Mr. and Mrs. Edwin Whiting; Jeffrey P. and Cynthia Whiting of East Barre; Miss Barbara Mills of Middlebury; Charles A. Whiting and Mr. and Mrs. Milton Hunt of Burlington; Mr. and Mrs. John O. Campbell of Montpelier; Mr. and Mrs. C.A. McCain and sons of Highgate Center.

When they came to Norwich, Miz Cross remembered, it was the Depression. Her salary for the school year was $700. Harold did odd jobs because regular jobs were hard to find. They were better off when Harold went to work for Trumbull-Nelson, builders across the Connecticut River in Hanover. After several years in an apartment, Harold built them a house outside the village center, right where the New Boston Road branches off from the Turnpike. Later, they bought a square white house behind the Norwich Inn in the village. Today the house has a sign in front of it: "The Marion W. Cross House." As time went on Harold grew sick and couldn't work. He died in 1965.

"I was lonesome as a dog when we got to Norwich, even with Harold," Miz Cross said. "We had an apartment in Robert Olds's house. They were good people and later on Bessie Olds taught for me, but it was so much different from being part of the town in Union Village, with the warmth of the large Gould family around me." After teaching fifth and sixth grades for three years, Miz Cross took over the seventh and eighth, and about then, no one seems to recall just when, she became the "Teaching-Principal." The south windows of her new room looked across the playground-town common to Main Street and across it to Joe Goodwin's house. Her room's west windows looked upon the White Church and the elm-shaded houses along Church Street, which also was U.S. Route 5 north toward Canada and south toward the outer world. My sister, Shirley, was in Miz Cross's first year teaching eighth grade before she went on to Hanover High School and thence to life as a doctor.

Miz Cross said that Norwich was a good town to teach in and that teaching in rural schools had seasoned her for a school four times as large as Union Village—although her own seventh and eighth grade pupils totaled about the number in all eight grades in Union Village. But not everything about the job was roses, especially at first. Charles Judd, a burly, dour man with a mustache thick as a rug, was the janitor. (He was the town clerk when I got to Norwich.) Mr. Judd fired the wood furnace that heated the school. He would leave his house grudgingly on chilly mornings to add logs, and then only after she had sent a message to him that everyone's teeth were chattering. "Then he took to locking the door to the furnace to save wood. He saved more money that way." After school was out he'd return to check whether lights had been left on, challenging teachers with being wasteful had they been remiss in switching them off. "Mary (Mrs.) Judd for years was a member of the school board. Every penny had to be accounted for. She kept us from having anything we wanted, most of the time, allowing us the bare necessities. But she had a good mind. I'd take her any day over Hattie Johnson."

Hattie was a miserable character, she recalled. "She was on the school board and always stirring up trouble. Hattie thought that the rural children ought to stay in their one-room schools—especially the Beaver Meadow school, which she thought her responsibility—and not be consolidated in the Norwich village school. She had it in for me because she believed I'd pushed her out of teaching seventh and eighth grades in the village school and because I would not use her very often as a substitute teacher. When I had to, it would take me a time to get pupils back in line after she left. She wouldn't send her son to me to school. She didn't like my teaching, and I didn't like hers." I asked Miz Cross if Hattie and Mary Williams, another vocalist on school affairs, were still around. She erupted with laughter: "They died," she said.

My mother tangled with Hattie in a PTA meeting. Newly come from New Jersey, my mother had joined, believing she should be civically responsible. At one meeting, the subject of the children's chairs and desks came up. These were yellow oak, fliptop, with a groove for pencils at the top and an inkwell in the top right corner. Chairs were separate and yellow oak and sturdy. I sat on these chairs and at these desks for eight years and can't recall their being uncomfortable. My mother seems to have thought they were and recommended getting more comfortable ones. Hattie squelched her: "They ain't goin to be comfortable all their lives, why should they be comfortable naow" (rhymes with meow). My mother accepted defeat and decided she and the PTA were a poor fit. No more meetings for her. Miz Cross's opinion, expressed to me, that the desks and chairs were not comfortable, didn't budge the PTA. I suspect that she didn't press the matter.

Hattie was married to W.O. Johnson, who had a reputation for "dealing" in real estate. Not a few in town thought they deserved each other. W.O. Johnson's property transactions were the subject of more than a little merriment. One winter, according to local lore, he sold a meadow with a nice stand of young pine to C.C. Hills, another village property dealer. Come spring, the snow melted, and the pines toppled over. They had been stuck in the snow.

Relations with school board members had been a considerable part of Miz Cross's duties. She thought that on the whole they had been effective and cordial. In her early years as principal, members were mostly concerned with school expenses. "If we asked for more money or supplies, they usually provided them. That didn't apply to salaries. I'd say we all need raises; they'd say, 'We know.'" During the Depression, the school board hired teachers at thirteen dollars a week. Old timers on the board came to school mostly if some child had been sent home for misbehaving. "They wanted to find out what was the trouble with the teacher."

As time passed, board members became more interested in what went on in school. Few had any knowledge about what a teacher should be teaching, and they'd come visit. As time went on, Miz Cross said, and as more doctors and professors and "city folks"—and parents intending to send their children to college—moved into town, board members increasingly became involved in school policy. Leslie Dewing came to teach music, the Dartmouth treasurer's wife was hired to teach French, and later there was an art teacher. Miz Cross said that she didn't recall much tension between the newer board members and the old timers, but the latter "wondered if the board needed to spend so much time talking about academic affairs."

The board and the superintendent of schools, Courtney Parker, hired the teachers, explained Miz Cross, and, to my astonishment, she did not interview the candidates and had no say in the hiring decision. On rare occasions, Mr. Parker consulted her about a candidate. With the exceptions of Mrs. Dewing and the French teacher, who Miz Cross had interviewed, she never met a teacher until after the teacher had been hired.

Leslie Dewing taught music once a week when I was in the seventh and eighth grades. I thought these were her first years, but Miz Cross said she had started earlier. Anyway, Mrs. Dewing was a marvel. I've told before how she'd appear in the room's door, elfin-like, dressed in a brown sweater and a tweed skirt, fiddle case under her arm, the brightest of eyes gleaming through thick glasses below a fringe of hair. She had us—the most unsophisticated of kids—singing Handel and the song of Churchill's Harrow. We sang not too badly, and we loved it.

Without much prompting, Miz Cross resumed talking about the board, this time thinking about some of the members. Roy Knights had done well in business. Clayton Berry owned the grist mill in Lewiston (a Norwich hamlet). He was very opinionated, and miserable about pay. She had as little as possible to do with him. John Fraser was good tempered, very interested in school finances. Mrs. Fraser was agreeable: "She'd come right in if there were any questions." Alma Cloud was very good; she kept up with the times, Miz Cross thought. Bessie Olds was very good, having had years of teaching experience. Carol Barwood, whose husband managed the Nugget theater in Hanover, was good, too. "She thought teachers ought to be paid more. Finally she got teacher pay to be pretty decent." Phoebe Hodder, wife of the Episcopal minister, Leslie, who Miz Cross thought was great, came on the board in 1939. Their daughters came to the school.

I had my own memories of many of the school board members Miz Cross had mentioned—and in some instances their families. Bessie Olds was a round, motherly lady with her hair wound tightly around her head. She and husband Rob, Mr. and Miz to us youngsters, worked in Gill's store, he behind the soda fountain and she selling sundries. Carol Barwood was the mother of Lefty Barwood, with whom I played baseball. Roy Knights's son, Calvin, had a Sunday-paper route, delivering to far outlying farms. He drove the car and I trotted to stoops with the actual newspaper, making a tiny income. I knew John Fraser's two sons, Stuart and Duncan. The younger, Stuart, married Peggy Ammel, a classmate in grade school, whose father's place was below ours on Elm Street. Years later I bought a collie pup from Peggy. Duncan, the elder, played ball on the Norwich town team. When he was not batting he'd go to his car to "buy a little insurance," open the trunk and take a swig from a brown bottle. "Duncan was the brightest member of the family," Miz Cross thought. "He was wild as a hawk. He'd feed his mother and father the darndest line."

I turned the conversation to religion. "Was it ever a problem in school or in the town?" I asked. I could not remember that it had been. My chum, Chink LaPorte, was Roman Catholic, and the Beauchene brothers, also Catholics, were part of our group. "No," she answered. "We said the Lord's Prayer and saluted the flag every morning before class." She dismissed the Jehovah's Witness's unwillingness to stand and salute the flag. "I just let it go, paid no attention. But I think that if you come to public school you ought to do what's done in public school." She was very pleased that Father Hodder had asked Frank LaPorte to unveil the blue and gold starred flag hanging in the town hall to commemorate village men serving and killed in the war. As I look back, I suspect the absence of religious friction was due largely to the small number of faiths in town other than Protestants and the town's essential tolerance. A man and his family were judged on their general conduct and whether or not they were hard workers. Miz Cross couldn't remember parents objecting to a textbook on religious or other grounds. "It would take me a while to swallow much of that," she said.

Class distinctions seemed to enter school life very little. On the playground, if you played sports hard and could hold up your end in a fight, you were OK. In the classroom, there could be an attitude akin to class, and some town and gown sentiment existed among adults, which the State Guard helped to overcome, thought Miz Cross. "Professors and doctors got to know farmers and other villagers and each found the other to be good people." For a while kids from Norwich village looked askance at kids bused in from the rural schools. Miz Cross commented about this. "Some village parents and their children looked down their noses at children from the country," she said, "but there were bright children, and village children could learn from them—as you did,

Granville, when the Hodgdon boy from Beaver Meadow beat you in arithmetic."

When I told my father about this cataclysmic event, he said, "Think of that!" I heard the tone and got the point. (Charlie Hodgdon stopped school with the eighth grade. His father needed him on the farm.)

Norwich began consolidating its school system in 1940-41, initially bringing in the seventh and eighth graders from the five rural, one-room schools: New Boston, Beaver Meadow, Turnpike, Root District, and Pompanoosuc. "Bringing in the older children eased the transition," Miz Cross said. "No doubt the school board had a job convincing the rural parents. Those people hated to lose their schools, and the children were uneasy about coming in to the village. Parents and pupils in those close communities both looked on the schools as theirs. Bringing the children a long way on buses could be hard on them. And the rural children wouldn't be able to stay after school and play. This would have eased integrating rural and village children, especially boys. Baseball is a leveler."

Busing at first was an awful nuisance, she remembered. Waiting in line was all right. Once on the bus there could be trouble, especially if in a rural area a couple of families were not getting along. The Brigham boys and others fought a lot. The two lady drivers were better than men at keeping the peace, children paid more attention to them. But Comery Cook had been good. He drove a school bus for years. "If things weren't right, he'd stop that bus and straighten them out." She thought for a while that she might have to ride one to keep order. She was glad she didn't have to. Comery Cook died a few years ago at age 105.

Continuing her remembrances about consolidation, Miz Cross said, "Stella Sears had taught for years in Beaver Meadow. She loved it, and it was the best school in the system. Stella was a great person. Her coming to teach in the village gave the people out there confidence. Stella didn't have a pleasant voice, she was stern looking, and she was quick tempered, but everything was done, everything corrected. She was fair and a natural instructor, a cracker-jack. I expect she was mother much of the time out there, although she didn't have too many motherly traits. The village children here were scared to death of her at first, but at the end of the year they realized they'd had a good one and learned a lot. On the first day the rural children came in here, you could tell those who had had Stella as a teacher. When they came to my seventh grade, they knew what they needed to know. At first Stella boarded with me and went back to Beaver Meadow on weekends."

Miz Cross stared out the window for a time, then smiled and turned to me. "One day I was standing at the window watching the Beaver Meadow children arrive. I saw this tall, long-legged boy coming along slowly, and even at that distance I could see he had a bouquet of flowers in his hand. Oh, glory be, I thought, he's bringing them for me." Chuckling, she continued, "I dashed down stairs as fast as

I could and went to him. I could see he was tickled to see me. 'I want you to have these flowers,' he said. I think I saved him a terrible ragging."

She returned to teaching. She'd always thought that a full day of school was enough for her and for the children. So keeping a child after school didn't achieve much. If a child couldn't function during the day, she asked, why could he function after four o'clock in the afternoon? Besides, if a child has had a full day in school, she said, he needs something else at the end of it, music, baseball.

It wasn't wise to press a child too hard if he wasn't interested, Miz Cross had found. That would turn him off. "Yet," she said, "children need to learn fundamentals, and I loved teaching English just as I had when I started out. It sounds antique these days, but I stressed simple English and writing sentences. Children have a lot to offer. They have imagination. They know more than you give them credit for. Draw them out. Set examples: bring in something good and read to them. I never set a reading list, but I'd ask for a list of what pupils had been reading." (My own list amounted to reading inflation.) "I believed in letting a child go ahead if he was ready—maybe give him a hint or two. A child might be thinking ahead and ask hard questions. If I couldn't answer I'd say so and say I'd be glad to talk with you about it."

"Testing: we had our own ideas about that. We didn't give tests in the primary grades, only from the fifth grade upwards. Teachers mostly made up their own tests according to the subject. We did use tests from some of the mathematics companies, not the Educational Testing Service. We wanted to see ourselves how the children were learning, and we didn't have to wait for the end of the school year to see which students were failing to learn. Teachers would discuss the results, which we didn't publicize, with each child. If I had given a test or a child had written a paper, I'd go over it with him. A set curriculum for each grade helps monitor pupils' progress. Now too much emphasis is given to testing. I don't think a test should be the thing on which a pupil is graded. Intelligence tests are bad because they don't allow for the child's background."

"Spelling is another thing. You have to realize that some people just can't spell, never will be able to. You can't make a child spell. But I'd teach it, and I got very upset when a teacher couldn't spell. One of them I had to get after all the time."

Here came another pause for coffee and, this time, her own chocolate chip cookies. I listened as she resumed, each of us catching the crumbs in our hands.

"Speaking good English could be a problem. Some teachers spoke poor English because they'd heard it and hadn't done enough correct speaking when they went to school. Emma McDonald was very, very good teaching third grade, but I did think she chewed up the English language some. Today there is so much bad English on television and radio that it's a wonder anybody speaks properly. Dialect and interesting sayings can be different."

Parents are a teacher's business, too, Miz Cross empha-sized, although she thought this so obvious it seemed silly to say it. A teacher ought to know something about each pupil's family, especially in Norwich where a teacher had to deal with big differences among parents—like those between the professors at Dartmouth and the doctors at the Hitchcock hospital and the town's rural families. The formers' children were not necessarily the brightest, but their background could be an advantage. Yet it wasn't simple. Did they have a bad or a good experience at home? Some parents were interested in their child and the school; others were not. Even well-educated parents, she said, being busy, might not give their children much attention. They might feed their children a good breakfast, "probably handmade," and put them on the bus. A child might not get as much attention as he ought to get. Teachers should know as much about this as they can.

"Parents of a child who was not learning," Miz Cross remembered, "might blame it on the teacher and lack of discipline. I often wondered if some of this criticism came from parents who were not doing enough for their own children. An average family can do a lot for a child. I always encouraged teachers to talk with parents. When they didn't want to, I suggested they have the parents get in touch with me. Children in some families had a more expansive vocabulary. Others didn't hear good English from four in the afternoon till nine the next morning. You have to talk sympathetically with parents. Many don't realize that a child can be different at home and at school. After the schools were consolidated occasionally there were stories about 'difficult' rural children. Mostly they weren't true. Some children just plain are slow learners. And parents don't always think about how tales grow between school and the supper table."

After she became unofficial school principal, Miz Cross found more time to work with other teachers, for example visiting classrooms. "After I was made principal I would go into a classroom and walk around the back while teaching continued," she said. "Watching the children told me about the teacher. I was so glad I'd had experience teaching all eight grades in rural school. This meant I could understand what was going on and how to help the teacher if she needed it. We had heard little about education 'philosophy' at Johnson, so we learned as we went along. Perhaps that's better than too much emphasis on 'philosophy'. Our teachers at Johnson taught us from their experience." She led teachers' meetings once a month to exchange ideas—with a fixed agenda, if possible, to save time. She preferred teachers who were not always in agreement with her and with each other and teachers who brought their problems and interests to the meetings. Keeping order usually was discussed. If a teacher had a problem, Miz Cross would talk with her individually. The other teachers taught her a lot, she remembered. She tried to learn good things about each teacher, but there were a few she was not sorry to see leave.

Having been the sole teacher for eight grades in rural schools and teaching only two grades in Norwich, Miz Cross had developed ideas about children having multiple teachers, as in most schools today. "Pupils may learn more about a subject from a teacher who specializes in it," she said. "No teacher is going to be equally good about everything. But if there is one teacher, children get to know her, and she knows them. This may have something to do with how settled they are. I think that a teacher especially for science or music or art is a good idea for children eighth grade and under."

Miz Cross didn't credit herself for all her ideas about teaching. She paid tribute to Superintendent of Schools Courtney Parker. He had been a big help to her over many years as a teacher and as a principal. She praised him as intelligent, well educated, and a fine person. He loved children. He was gentle. He talked well with parents, especially ones whose child was in some kind of difficulty. He advised her to be tolerant even of those children "who drive you up the wall."

"He made me have more respect for children, good, bad, or indifferent. It was the indifferent ones I worried about. He knew more about teaching than many other superintendents. Those would come in, stand around, and leave, not do much for the school. 'Remember, Marion' he would say 'present the children with ideas and see how they take them and this will tell you how well they can learn.' And he'd say 'Let children learn. Don't talk to them all the time.' He was fifteen years ahead of his time. He advised me 'keep children in hand while still befriending them. Some children willfully won't mind. Talk to them, including to the parents if need be. Set your rules. Parents can be very sensitive about this, even if they don't treat their own children very well. You can learn a lot about the child by knowing about the parents.'"

Once a month Mr. Parker would visit each room in the school to see how the teachers he had interviewed were doing. At a later teachers meeting, he would talk about what he'd observed. School board members relied on him to keep track of the school, they knowing little about what, or how, a teacher should be teaching. The superintendents for Vermont met once a year, school boards also yearly, in Montpelier.

Despite Miz Cross's appreciation of Mr. Parker, as a pupil I saw him as an ominous figure, with a longish face, slim in a gray double-breasted suit. For no reason I can now discern, the room seemed chilly with him present. Maybe it was a guilty conscience. Hamlet knew what he was talking about.

Miz Cross never conveyed to me, or, I think, to others, a sense of doom-in-waiting. She, herself, was the reason. No one was afraid of her, but you knew that if you acted up, you'd be in trouble—at a minimum impaled on a piercing look. Quiet, friendly, always approachable, she had an aura: what she said was law. She was beyond challenge—perhaps because she never lifted a finger to be thought so.

She reminds me of the Archibald MacLeish line, "A poem must not mean, but be." Miz Cross just was.

After her retirement, Miz Cross continued to carry an aura of distinction. Townspeople liked her, and "I always liked people awfully well. Most of them," she added. "Of course, I knew so many people and they'd talk to me, just casual meetings. I'm glad Dan and Whit's was so full of people. (This is Norwich's famous general store, for years Merrill's General Store.) I could go cross lots and have company, although my back scared me. (She had fallen off a chair when changing a light bulb.) Even though I wasn't teaching I felt part of the town." What she was too reticent to say was that she, and the other longtime teachers in town, were leading citizens. They had not reached this status overnight—only if they had taught the children seriously and sought the parents' understanding for what they were doing.

Teaching, teachers, the school, and the town had changed a great deal since the writer was a pupil, Miz Cross said. They teach more American history now. More is done with Latin roots of English. Hanover school teachers had told her that Norwich children, when they came over for high school, know more English grammar than Hanover children. (Today, children go to Hanover starting with the seventh grade; the Norwich school stops with grade six.) Yet she wondered if in her day they had taught the principles of grammar too much. Had this interfered with writing interesting articles? She thought the special music, science, and art teachers had been a success, and the French teacher as well. She sensed that the younger parents were paying more attention to the school. She was glad about this, for it seemed to have improved quality in the younger grades.

When a plan to add a new building to the original school was put forward, it aroused ill feeling. "The idea took an awful licking in the town," she recalled. This had worn off since 1950, and she was pleased that the new building had more single-grade rooms, permitting greater attention to each child. She purposely had stayed out of things, she said, but when teachers invited her in for special programs, she could see that things were going well. The teachers get better salaries, now the best in the area, she thought. Best of all, the new people in town, some of whom may have thought they could improve it, had failed to swamp the older residents.

Marion Cross retired from teaching the June after the March 1973 town meeting that had named the school after her. Townspeople didn't think she or her colleague, Stella Sears, should be allowed to go quietly. Miz Sears had stood for as many years as Marion Cross before attentive—and they'd better be!—children. In April, the invitations went out to come to the town hall on May 13, two to five in the afternoon, for a reception in honor of the two teachers. It would be an "occasion of sadness," the invitation read, "but...reason for a genuine expression of our friendship and gratitude for what they have done for this town and our children." The day, a Sunday, also was Mother's Day. The newspaper photos showed the two ladies all smiles sitting in chairs, and Miz Cross, in a skirt, white blouse, and a button-up sweater, standing to speak to the guests. "I remembered everybody except one," she told me with satisfaction.

Former school superintendents and representatives of other school districts attended. The *Hanover Gazette* reported that four hundred attended the party in the town hall. Eunice Gilman wrote the story for the *Gazette*. (Eunice and husband, Lee, had been hired man and wife for my parents during the Forties. They lived on the third floor of our house, and Eunice and my mother developed a deep friendship. Lee was a friendly, although taciturn, man, good to me. I remember how his scrawny arms did not reveal his great strength. Several hundred pounds was nothing to him.) The hall had been decorated with pine boughs and spring flowers. The refreshment committee, chaired by Virginia Porter, served sandwiches and drinks. "Mrs. Carl Kelly made a cake for the occasion in the shape of the Norwich school," Eunice reported. Al Foley—professor at Dartmouth, sometime moderator of town meetings and teller of Vermont stories in dialect—presided.

The Norwich Quartet "sang some old-time songs," Eunice continued. Jim Southworth led a group in singing *Forty Years On*—the Harrow School song that Leslie Dewing had taught Jimmy and me when we were pupils. (Jimmy was doing well with his Subaru agency on the road to White River Junction.) The retirees received gifts and scrapbooks with messages and pictures "as a remembrance of the occasion," wrote Eunice.

Just at the end of the school year, on the afternoon of May 30, the school's children put on a more elaborate program in the town hall, a "Musical Program" the mimeographed sheet called it. The "Presentation of the Colors" began the proceedings. The Honor Guard brought in "the new Marion W. Cross School flag." The Pledge of Allegiance, the *Star Spangled Banner*, and the Alma Mater followed. Choral selections came next; then a narration accompanied by the fifth and sixth grade band; then piano and flute solos and finally a piano duet and a "Charleston Dance" featuring I. Munck, T. Wallis, C. James, K. Seibert, K. Lofgren, and A. Valtin. Then came two selections from Bach cantatas, plus medleys, presentations, and *Bye, Bye, Mrs. Marion Cross* to the tune of *American Pie*, sung by the combined sixth grades with B. Miller on the guitar. A queen could not have had better.

Newspaper articles carried praises. "She always had a smile on her face, yet you knew you couldn't get away with much," said Polly Rand, a pupil from my generation. "You always knew you could go to her. You knew she was there and she was the final say." Donald Ballam, a schoolmate of mine, also recalled having to toe the mark. But "if you needed help or if you were having trouble with other things she would go out of her way to help you." He remembered her as "quite a sport...If you were doing something, she would join in no matter what it was." Fran Stone, who taught for Miz Cross for seventeen years, thought Miz Cross was far ahead of her time. "She thought everybody was worth listening to." Math teacher John Girard thought community respect for her "came from her very strong character." Teaching under her was "a terrific experience for me...She helped me become a good teacher."

Marion Cross died in December 1996. At her funeral, Norwich residents and friends filled the White Church to overflowing. Teachers and students gathered between the town hall and the church and sang, standing on the bare ground. Snow came late that year.

CHAPTER ELEVEN

SEVERAL MEN

Heads are nodded and shaken in various ways in different cultures to convey various sentiments. Norwich is one of these cultures. For instance, a nod with the chin going down recognizes an individual who is either a friend or a familiar acquaintance. Conversely, tipping the chin up when meeting a person acknowledges his presence without expressing warmth nor coolness—perhaps only indifference. If two persons encounter each other, and do not exchange nods of either sort, they are strangers or they are unfriendly. The chin-down nod may be through your and the other person's windshield as your cars pass each other. A wave will do, or an index finger lifted off the steering wheel. Meeting a lady on the street, a man likely would speak a greeting, first name if familiar or Hello, Miz so-and-so. Such communication suits terse Vermonters.

Spoken language salutations are more difficult to categorize. Norwich boasted no protocol, and few generalizations apply. Yet a degree of delicacy was important. Length of acquaintance and friendliness allowed me to call a much older man like Will Bond by his first name. I called Hazen Stickney, Hazen, although I didn't know him awfully well, and he was a contemporary of Charlie DeVaux—whom I addressed as Mister. I called the town clerk, Robert Fitzgerald, Rob, although he was 30 years older than I, but I would never have called his father, Fred Fitzgerald, the town sheriff/constable, Fred—although he took me on a companionable fishing trip to the Connecticut Lakes. I addressed my friends' fathers as Mister or Doctor, not as Professor. Why? I guess I simply absorbed the code. Maybe it's like French, some words you don't pronounce the way they're spelled. You just have to know their peculiarities.

For instance, I called Jim Aldrich, a generation older than I, Jim. He lived on a small place out of Norwich village. He was slender, wiry, had unruly hair, and often needed a shave. He cut and sold pulp-grade wood for newsprint and hired out to the town for work on the roads. A line in the Town Report often would read, "Jim Aldrich and truck," so many dollars for so many hours. One year at town meeting the selectmen appointed him road commissioner, and Jim worked hard at the most thankless job in town. In every season someone had a complaint about their road as though they were the only soul living on it: plowing, ruts in mud time, and washboards. Jim listened to the gripes and kept working. His diligent efforts kept the town moving on its nearly one hundred miles of mostly-dirt road. I never saw him mad. ("Not mad, Granville, angry," Miz. Cross would have interjected.)

I addressed Maurice Aldrich, descendant of a line of cabinet makers, as Mister. He had a soft, gray voice and comfortably filled his soft, gray suits. A kindly man, he had the avuncular jowls of the successful banker he was. As a selectman and chairman of the town's finance committee, he made many contributions to town governance. Why was he a Mister? It may have been the gray suits and the avuncular manner. Or was it because he was a town selectman alongside my father?

Roy Aldrich had a blind deer that was better known than he was. Roy kept it penned for some years in his backyard on Mechanic Street. He would lead it around the village on a halter, his pockets full of apples for children to feed it. One day, out of the blue, the pet reared up and attacked Roy with its front hooves, which could split your skull. Unwilling to return the blind animal to the forest, Roy shot it.

As a game warden, Roy Aldrich, who always wore high boots, was a power in Norwich and other areas where his authority extended. He had a belief in the law and reputation for fairness and decency. I addressed him as Roy, as many did. His reputation didn't restrain Benny Tuttle, who must have been feeling good, from shooting a hole in his hat. Roy was about to cite Benny for fishing in the reservoir, not for the first time, which was prohibited. Benny had a determined streak in him. One time when a friend was visiting him—probably to collect stories—the telephone rang one long and two shorts. "Isn't that your ring," the friend asked?

"I put that telephone in for my convenience," Benny replied. "I'll answer it when I want to."

Would you have guessed that the Aldriches were brothers?

———

Leon Merrill, another man I called Mister, owned Merrill's Store on Main Street. It had been named A.H. Merrill Co. when his father owned it. Leon worked there daily. He was tallish, firmly built, and balding. His expression was more sober than stern. You had to decide if he had smiled. A man once said of him, "Leon don't give much away, but he don't ask for nothin', neither." My only run-in with him was when he called me into his office after one Halloween and accused me of writing with a candle on his display windows. He had me, for Betty Barrett had tattled. I had to clean the windows, but there were no hard feelings. The store sold everything in Leon's time—from soap to shovels—and there were Texaco gas pumps out front. People stopped there almost as regularly as they breathed.

When Leon Merrill wanted to retire, he sold the store to Dan Fraser and Whit Hicks, who had worked for him for years. Whit was just plain jolly. Dan was a strong, no-nonsense man with a sense of humor. I called them both by their first names. Dan heated his house with wood and fueled the store's furnace with it, the heat rising through a large round iron register in the floor. Long racks of two-foot wood for his house and the store filled his back yard. "Dan and Whit's," as it is now named, is renowned far beyond Norwich. It sells even more now than in Mr. Merrill's day, both in the main store and in a galvanized shed out back, filled with farm tools and hardware supplies. Dan and Whit began selling beer and wine soon after they took over the store, which Leon Merrill would not do—even during those years when the town was wet. Later they began selling wine with their own label, whose chalet on it shows their names, but omits the gas pumps. Sadly, Whit is now gone; Dan is in a nursing home and still a great storyteller. A few years ago twee individuals unknown to me suggested renaming the place The Country Store. They must have been from away.

Glen Merrill was as tall as Leon. Gangly with a round head on a longish neck, he seemed taller. He walked with a lively step. As the Moderator at town meeting for several years, his drollery turned away much wrath. An officer in the Dartmouth National Bank, he was as cheery as his colleague there, Maurice Aldrich, was grave. The town benefitted from the presence of both Leon and Glen, but Glen was the one you'd invite to dinner. I addressed him as Glen.

They, too, were brothers.

—————

Chief Hollicy, if I recall his name correctly, was chief of police in Hanover. I, and everyone else, called him Chief. Preceded by his blue belly straining at its gold buttons, he strode the sidewalks and directed traffic ponderously. As citizens said, "Thinks he's some punkins, don't he."

Coming upon a largish excavation in Main Street one day, in front of where the Dartmouth Bookstore is now, he leaned over the temporary barrier. "What you diggin' foah?," he asked in that my-good-man tone.

Man in the hole replied, "Thutty cents an ahwah," and went on digging. I don't know if either man had a brother.

———

Bert Cloud, who I called Mister, stood tall and bony at his over 80 years. His eyes were dimming, and when he drove a car down Main Street, those who saw him coming took refuge behind the nearest maple trunk. He was grandfather to my school mate, Harry. After years on the family farm—as I recall up the hill off to the left from the New Boston church—Bert decided to look for smaller quarters in the village, "One of them places with steam heat," he said. Dale Nelson, a builder and partner in Trumbull-Nelson Company, the lumber yard in Hanover (Dale to me), owned a two-family house on Norwich Main Street—one apartment downstairs, the other up.

Bert looked over the upstairs apartment and pronounced it tolerable, but too small. "'I bought me an organ and their ain't room for it,'" he told Dale, who was annoyed. Maybe he thought Bert pretentious. Somewhat later, Bert took himself a wife, and soon thereafter, as Dale related, "I met him in front of Merrill's Store. I says to him, Bert, got a place for your organ naow, ain't ya.?"

———

Deacon Douglas and Doctor Jones lived almost across from one another on Main Street. Each had a barn behind his house—the Deacon for a half dozen cows and the Doctor for the horse that pulled his buggy for house calls. As a youngster, I knew them by sight, but I never spoke to either. Stories about them were plentiful and went back many years.

Doctor Jones spoke seldom and was remembered as a common-sense practitioner who made house calls in any weather. His horse made him famous. The beast took to lying down between the buggy shafts, causing the doctor frustration and costing him time to rouse the horse and get him pulling. One day, just after breakfast, when the horse lay down where the doctor's driveway joined the street, the doctor lost patience. He climbed down from the seat, walked to the horse's head and sat on it. He called for pipe and tobacco and puffed serenely, unmoved by the horse's protests. Come noon, so the story goes, Doc Jones stood up and so did the horse. Doc never had to repeat the performance.

Deacon Douglas was a small, slightly bent man with iron-gray hair. I remember him sprightly trotting along Main Street behind his cows, now and then whacking one companionably on the rump with his stick. Townspeople must have found the cow pies irksome, for after a while the Deacon sold his small herd. One day he was in Gill's store enjoying a soda when a man began profanely berating his horse. The Deacon admonished him that it was all right to swear at oxen, "but you ought never swear at a hoss."

————

 I met Hazen Stickney through the DeVaux family. I called him Hazen, although he was Mr. DeVaux's age and coworker as road patrolman on Route 5. Why Hazen was an exception to the code, I can't imagine. But there it is. This man was a hard worker, jolly, thickset without being rotund, and a good shot with a rifle. With his old Colt forty-five revolver, he was a marvel. He would aim for so long, you thought his arm would fall off from the strain. When he did shoot, you knew that whatever he was aiming at was dead.

 Hazen told a story this way.

 He had to contend with a fox that was a miracle of wiliness. He did not set out on a stormy night, praying for a moon to give him light. He flaunted his skills, operating by day as well as by night. Despite Hazen's continuous efforts in self-defense—or in his chickens' and ducks' defense—he lost birds to him. Try as he might, Hazen had never got a shot at him, and he refused to trap him. Like a partridge, the fox had to be killed on the wing, fairly. But no hound dog could keep up with him nor put him across the road where a hunter, ever so wise in fox lore, could predict and wait for him in ambush. This fox was above the lore.

 Come March with the new chicks due, Hazen told most everyone that he was sick of that fox. What to do?

What to do was a dead deer. Wounded by an out-of-season hunter, it collapsed in the snow one evening and died in the field a hundred yards below Hazen's house. Hoping the fox would come for a sniff, Hazen sat himself at his open kitchen window before dawn—cup of coffee on the table, Krag rifle on the sill, cocked and the sights set.

The fox did come by, Hazen later related, "an I took a bead an I shot. That fox jumped right up inta the air, an he mustuv run a hundred yaads before he come down. I walked down to see how much I'd missed him by. I'd shot jest under him. There was a yellow streak in the snow. Naow, I've heard of scaring the piss out of somebody, but I never seen it before."

CHAPTER TWELVE

No Probation

People from away who settled in Norwich were welcomed, tacitly, provided they accepted and accommodated to the town's rich and ancient culture and were reticent with their opinions. People from away included those from New Hampshire, southern Vermont, Boston, or New York, city or state. Like children, they should be seen and rarely heard. This probation lasted an indeterminate period. I recall when Fred Johnson, a piano tuner, who was liked after ten years in town, mentioned in town meeting an idea that "we newcomers recommend." Well, he'd lost right there. The meeting tossed it out as quick as a short trout.

Father Leslie Hodder seemed never to go through a probationary period, or, if so, it was very short. Lacking a drop of Episcopalian blood, I still addressed him as Father. Townspeople took this slender, slightly stooped, English Episcopalian priest to their hearts, although the faithful mostly attended the Congregational "White Church" across the common. St. Barnabas, in the village, was his home church, and he also observed Vespers summer Sunday evenings in the old one-room, unpainted once-Methodist church in Beaver Meadow—a four-house, four-corners hamlet five miles west of the village. He continued to conduct services in both Norwich churches after he had been given St. Thomas Church across the Connecticut River in Hanover.

His family was equally liked. When a villager asked if he was a self-made man, Father Hodder replied, "No, I'm the revised product of a wife and two daughters." The daughters went to grade and high school with us, and Polly, a proper tomboy, played tackle football on the common-cum-schoolyard, which was conveniently centered between the two churches, in case of fatalities.

Telling stories on himself was one of Father Hodder's winning ways. Beaver Meadow figured in two of these. On a rise in one of the four corners stood a tired looking house inhabited by an old couple living untidily. They had as housekeeper a lady, casual of figure and dress, who kept a half-dozen mongrel dogs. One evening, having decided that he should make a pastoral visit, Father Hodder left his car by the side of the road, fitted himself between strands of rusty barbwire, and started up the rise. In the yard the dogs clamored. Their mistress came to the door, identified the visitor, and, according to Father Hodder, hollered, "Goddam yeh shut up! Don't you know there's a minister comin'?"

Driving to and from Vespers, Father Hodder for weeks had admired a farmer's flower garden. Seeing a man hoeing in it one evening, he pulled over, got out, and leaned over the fence. "We talked for a while," Father remembered, "and I told him that I thought his flowers were beautiful. 'You ought to thank the Good Lord for this garden.' I said. He looked at me for a time and said, 'Parson, you shoulda seen this piece when the Almighty had it to himself.'"

For two, maybe three, years before the war, Father Hodder turned dramatist. He mustered performers, stage hands, and other villagers in staging old fashioned minstrel shows. Ernest Fitzgerald and Harold Kingsbury were co-interlocutors. They also sang, the latter with a strong bass, Mr. Fitzgerald with a fine baritone. He also did a nimble soft shoe dance. Mike Bean, cook in our State Guard company, wowed the hall by singing "I love the bearded lady 'cause her whiskers tickle so." Roars shook the hall as the endmen told jokes on their fellow townsmen—many made up by Father Hodder, the audience suspected. I regret that only a few of these are still with me.

One was that a doctor had been seen making a hurried call to the Metcalf farm on Metcalf Hill, where bode the siblings Abbie, Paul, and Fred. Could it have been a maternity case?

Roar.

Jane Ballam had been agitating her husband to go with her to the White Church. Finally, he capitulated *if* she promised to rouse him gently. She settled on onions and, Sunday morning having arrived, she waved a bunch under his nose. Stirring, Warren said, "Jane get your feet off my pillow."

Roar.

There was a joke about me, probably because I was coltish about his daughter Polly.

The singing and the songs were good. Within days, the jokes were told and retold in every corner of the town.

CHAPTER THIRTEEN

A Meeting at Jack Cray's

"Had my oil changed," Bill announced cheerfully, just having returned from the hospital and the latest transfusion barely keeping his leukemia at bay. I had made this particular trip to Bill because his wife, Lil, had telephoned saying that I'd better hurry. He would be dead in a few weeks. He stood in the middle of his shop, hand resting casually on the back of a chair, the racks along the walls empty of the guns that had filled them. Bill looked well, a bit taller than his normal six feet. The shop was still; we just looked at each other.

William J. DeVaux and I often wondered how we met. We never resolved the question, although we settled provisionally on Jack Cray's, with our common age then about twelve. Jack ran a small store in a log cabin on Route 5, halfway between Norwich Village and Pompanoosuc. He had two Gulf gas pumps out front and inside sold groceries, and bought, sold, and traded guns. He had a small shooting range beside the store, which, for safety's sake, faced the wooded ridge behind the store. Jack was a short, stocky man, age approaching sixty. His filling-station cap covered thinning gray hair. He wore a pleasant but noncommittal expression, smiling warmly for those he knew.

On weekends, he'd host pistol matches. In the fall, he'd have turkey shoots—the best score on the target won a turkey. Any day several men, fewer women, and a few Dartmouth students dropped by to buy or trade guns, to talk guns, to shoot, or for a gossip—about news and events, about the partridge population that year, or whether the lack of rain meant that the woods would be closed during deer season. If someone in these gatherings bragged about his shooting eye or steady hand, Jack would hand him a 22 rifle or a 20-gauge shotgun and say "Let's see you shoot." Failure brought the bragger's embarrassed departure. Jack was a good shot himself, and a fine coach for many of us. With my father's permission, I traded a long-barreled, single-shot Colt 22 for a Hi-Standard Model C 22 semi-automatic pistol (firing only 22 shorts) for target matches. The first match I shot was at Jack's. I found that I scored higher in rapid-fire than in slow-fire—maybe I shook too much in the latter. Whether or not Bill and I first met there, we met there often. "Let's see you shoot" became our response to anyone puffing himself up about anything.

We took to each other, and his family admitted me. Beyond my own family, a more rewarding association I cannot imagine. It was warm and embracing, jolly and kind beyond measure. I learned about the woods, about guns and shooting, about the great skill with a fly rod that I never achieved. The most lasting lesson of all has been how honest *dead honest* is, about how a family of very modest means can live decently and enjoy life without frills—and about the best chocolate cake I've ever tasted.

The DeVauxs were not the only upright family in town. There were many others. The community's culture said that individuals should *do right* by others. Work should be done well, debts paid, and prices fair. The lines of duty were clean and square, serene and lasting, like those of the federal houses on Main Street and the Congregational Church. I heard dark things hinted about a few townspeople, mostly as a result of faction fights, I now assume. But an individual's most valuable possession was a reputation for being straight.

The DeVauxs were a family of six. Father Charlie DeVaux, who I called Mister; mother Millie, who I called Miz DeVaux; Grampa Will Harrison, second husband to Mrs. Harrison, Charlie DeVaux's mother; and two sons, Alfred and Bill. Younger than Bill, Alfred and I never were close. Mr. Harrison seemed to me perpetually old. He was spry enough to help in the vegetable garden in summer. In winter, he observed the world with a dry expression while rocking by the big white kerosene stove, chewing the stem of his pipe. He said little, perhaps in reaction to Mrs. Harrison's volubility. What he did say could be amusing. I remember his account of his first conversation on the new-fangled telephone: "The bell rung, an I went over to the wall and put that horn-shaped thing to my ear and said hello. The other feller said hello, an I said hello, an he said hello, an I said hello, an I hung up."

Mrs. Harrison had a shrill kindness and seemed often to get on Millie DeVaux's nerves. I see Mrs. Harrison somewhat in the background in the kitchen, where we all spent much time, short and dumpy behind her apron, with a much wrinkled face and faded frizzy hair. She helped cook and wash up.

Miz DeVaux was tallish and husky in her plain dress, round faced, with a hearty voice and a laugh to match. She was a great cook, beyond her chocolate cake, and a good shot, tramping the hills after deer with her menfolk. She had arrived from Switzerland to sit unmet at Ellis Island, a girl alone. A priest helped her, arranging a trip to Connecticut and a job. The priest's faith is lost to history, but the DeVauxs, when in Norwich, went to the Episcopal church. Charlie DeVaux lived in the same area, working as a machinist. Of their courtship and early married life, I know nothing.

Charlie DeVaux headed the family effortlessly. His rumbly bass voice, with its undercurrent of good humor, seemed never to impose. Requests within the family were courteous. Slope-shouldered and strong, his gentle girth didn't slow him down on the flat or on the hill. He was a gunsmith who could fix almost anything, and a fine shot with revolver, rifle, and shotgun. Guns of various sorts filled the house, and Charlie kept a loaded 45 Smith and Wesson revolver hanging from the headboard of his bed.

In the DeVauxs' house, and in my own (and in the field, also) gun safety and gun manners were drilled into us and became our creed. We learned to be gentlemanly with guns. Clean and oil guns after use. No loaded guns in the house, excepting Mister's 45. Break shotguns while crossing fences. Never point a weapon, loaded or not, at anyone—accidentally or purposely. Never snap a hammer on an unloaded weapon—to avoid breaking the firing pin. Never fire unless you know where the bullet's going to stop. Immediately upon being handed a weapon, check that it is unloaded. Ditto when handing a weapon to someone. I cannot recall an accidental (or purposeful) wounding of one person by another, of any age, all the time I was growing up, although I did shoot myself in the leg with a 22 pistol when practicing a quick draw and hip shooting. The accident scared hell out of my father, who downed a Scotch before driving me to the hospital, but he realized I'd learned a lesson, and I continued gunning.

We loved guns, treated them carefully and respectfully, and tried to shoot more accurately. Bill and I talked ballistics—bullet weights and loads, the foot pounds of their hitting power, and mid-range trajectories—as avidly as other kids talked baseball statistics. A Red Sox and a Dimaggio fan, Bill also could talk baseball statistics. I loved playing baseball, but I didn't know which team was in which league.

Bill and I developed a relationship of companionable insult, regularly impugning each other's abilities and intelligence. We hunted, fished, and tramped all over. He shot better than I with rifle and pistol, although I could trail not too far behind him in our rifle matches with gun clubs in other towns. In the field he excelled with both rifle and shotgun.

One day we had hunted partridges on a south-facing slope in a warm October sun among crab apple trees in a deserted orchard. Walking lazily after a bird-less day, we were throwing apples at each other, ones the deer hadn't eaten. A bird roared up behind Bill. He whirled on one leg and got it. We fitted together gunning, for he was left handed and I right. I carried a long gun in the crook of my left elbow; he in the crook of his right. When walking side by side our weapons pointed away from the other.

Adding insult to injury, Bill was pools ahead of me with a fly. I'd fish a pool or riffle and declare it empty; he'd come along and take a 10-inch trout from it, often casting under low-hanging bushes to do it. I wish he could have fished the Big Blackfoot River with author Norman Maclean, his father and his brother. Which reminds me of one of the best sentences in the language—as good as Hemingway and E.B. White combined. Maclean said—in *A River Runs Through It*—that his preacher father was very sure about certain matters pertaining to the universe. Then: "To him, all good things—trout as well as eternal salvation—come by grace and grace comes by art and art does not come easy."

Bill and I, in the days before I could drive, travelled far in early hours in search of trout, with our rods

strapped to our handlebars, worms, flies, and lunch in
Boy Scout knapsacks. The roads to Thetford, Strafford,
and the distant reaches of Norwich may have been stony
or dusty, with long hills to push our bicycles up, but I
remember best the clover blossoms and the red-topped
grasses in the fields, and the cool green tunnels through
the woods. My mother gave me honey sandwiches for
lunch—plenty of honey, which soaked into the bread
and made it crunchy. I caught trout, but my memories
are less of the catches than of still, cool hours on streams,
with waters rippling over gray stones and warblers flit-
ting in the thickets.

During the late Thirties, farmers in Norwich were
finding crows and woodchucks more than usually annoy-
ing. The Norwich Fish and Game Club put a bounty on
them: five cents for a pair of crow's feet and five cents for
a woodchuck tail. Bill and I saw opportunity. By the end
of the summer we were not rich; our treasure sacks were
worth about a buck and a half each, and more than a bit
ripe. We alternated shots. One time, after stalking a woodchuck sunning himself on the mound of excavated earth
by his hole, we fell to arguing that it was the other fellow's
turn. We were no nearer resolution when a train whistling
in the valley below scared the chuck in. Question: how
much time will a woodchuck chuckle before chucking it
in? Bill's eyes were better than mine, my hearing better
than his. We were a good pair, he'd say. Alone, neither of
us was worth a damn.

Deer hunting was a family affair. All but the Harrisons participated. Sport surely, but more, for a couple of deer meant meat for the winter. Mrs. DeVaux preserved it in Mason jars, and it made delicious pot roast. Deer liver we ate fresh. Vermont law permitted one buck a person, and the carcass had to be registered at an official station. Years later, doe seasons were established when the state's herd grew too large for available feed. Some days we hunted in a rough line. In certain weathers, Mr. DeVaux divided our forces, some members hunting while at the same time pushing deer toward the others waiting in ambush by deer crossings. Stalking was best after rain or light snow had quieted the leaves.

There were ample pleasures in a day in the fields and woods, under and among pines and hemlocks, beech sap-lings, and late-shedding red maples, even if we came home empty handed. The air was fresh enough to bottle and sell—if Ganges water, why not Vermont air? Yet the same air could warn deer downwind of our presence. While trying to move soundlessly, we had to be alert for quarry betrayed in the motion of a bough or an out-of-the-ordi-nary shape or color among the hardwoods—where a deer's grayish autumn coat blends well. Mr. DeVaux called this skill hunter's eye—noting shapes or colors varying from the forest's pattern.

A silent What's that?, and then an anxious assessment: Was it a deer at all? Was it a buck? Could you see any horns? (We didn't say antlers.) Where would the bullet stop? With these calculations made in a blink or two of the eye—a deer's patience being limited—came either relaxation, for nothing was there among the saplings, or a quick shot aiming to kill not wound. A wounded animal would be trailed. A kill would be followed by field dressing and registering the carcass at the state inspection station. At home the deer was hung by the horns to drain and thereafter fully dressed to await canning when the meat was right. The deer hung, we discussed the hunt in weary contentment over hot tea and chocolate cake in the warm kitchen.

The DeVauxs had two houses, the first rented, the second bought. Kitchens in each heard reminiscences about hunts and stories of many kinds. The first kitchen, in the weather-worn but handsome federal-style house in which the family lived when I was first inducted into it, was up Route 5 from Jack Cray's, closer to Pompanoosuc. Among my memories are its worn linoleum floor, the kerosene and wood stoves (the latter for backup), the cupboards which needed painting against the far wall, the metal sink, and the huge breakfasts Mrs. DeVaux gave Bill and me when I slept over in order for us to get a good start on some adventure.

That was where I sassed Benny Tuttle, who was painting the kitchen. Benny was a jolly painter and, like so many at the time, had little money and occasionally shot a deer out of season to feed his family—using salt for bait. Everyone in town knew this, probably even the game warden, but no one minded because they, too, had trouble filling the pot. That day, Mrs. DeVaux had packed sandwiches for Billy and me, for we were after big game: woodchucks. When Benny saw these he said, "When I was a boy we didn't have no lunch given us. All we had was a fryin' pan an some salt." I retorted, "Yeah, Benny, but we puts salt on the meat after we shoots it." He laughed, and I escaped a boxed ear.

I also remember how startled I was on the first night I slept over when my bed shook as a train passed on the track just the other side of Route 5. These were steam trains and whistled the allure of distant places.

Mr. DeVaux had his machine and gun shop on the second floor of the shed attached to the back of the house. This had a chair by the rear window overlooking a nearby hill. From it, he sighted-in rifles and tried out loads. I was thrilled to watch him fire a 45/550 Sharps—Hopalong Cassidy's gun—roaring and belching smoke from the black powder loads.

The hamlet of Pompanoosuc—part of Norwich town with a store, a few houses, a primary school Bill attended until high school—was a couple of miles up Route 5 from the house. Beyond this stretched a long meadow, one of the intervales that made the valley so attractive to Indians and early settlers for growing corn. This meadow had been the site many years earlier of a legendary train wreck. Two trains, one travelling north, the other south, collided there. One farmer was the only eyewitness, and as such he was summoned to a hearing in Springfield, Massachusetts. The hearing judge, wiser than many, advised the man to take his time: "Just describe what you saw in your own words," he instructed.

The lore continues that the witness began, "Well, I got the chores done an hitched up my team an went to plowin' in that big medder. Pretty soon I hears a train whistle up the valley. There wahnt nothin' unusual 'bout that, a train usually come down 'bout that time. I plows a furrow goin' north an nother goin' south. Then I hears a train whistle from down the valley, and I thinks that's mighty peculiar. I looks way up the valley an I seen that southbound enjine coming into sight; then I looks way south and seen the same thing. 'Somethin's goin' to happen,' says I to myself. So I drives the team away from the track an over to where I kin set on a rock. Them two enjines come together with some awful crash. An I says to myself, 'ain't that a helluva way to run a railrud.'"

When the family lived in that house, Mr. DeVaux's regular income came from being a road patrolman. This meant driving his truck over an assigned stretch of Route 5 and keeping the verges mowed and tidy, the culverts and ditches open, patching bad spots in the macadam, fixing guard rails, repairing tourist tables and benches, and so on. He supplemented his income not only by gunsmithing but also by selling gas from two pumps beside the house. (These were gone by my time.) This was during Prohibition and Route 5 was an important smuggling route down from Canada to

New York. Often at night, Mr. DeVaux recalled, he'd be wakened by a honking in the yard and see a big sedan, with a big trunk strapped to the rear, stopped by the pumps. He'd go down and fill the tank for men with their coat collars up and their hat brims down. They'd pay and drive away, not a word spoken.

I asked if anyone had refused to pay. One night, he answered, "a feller starts to hand me the money an stops short of givin' it to me. 'What if I don't pay?' he says. I says, 'look up there,' an there was Millie in the window with a shotgun trained on him. By the time he looked back at me, I had a 45 in his belly. He said nothin'. Just gave me the money an drove off." It matters to no one except me that that revolver is mine today. Many years ago Mr. DeVaux sold it for $15. He needed the money.

The family left this house when the lease ran out and bought another closer to Norwich village. It was in sight of the Connecticut River and the black ridge of pines on the higher New Hampshire bank. It was closer to the railroad than the other house. A toddler could have tossed a stone from the front porch onto the tracks. River Road crossed the tracks some 50 yards away and trains hooted warning for the crossing, two longs and two shorts. I think the DeVauxs found the trains—few by then—companionable and their presence made the house cheaper to buy.

An additional advantage was that the house was within walking distance to Hanover High School thus making it easier for Bill to play sports. He pitched, until he threw his arm out, while I played third base. He also played basket-ball, which meant a winter walk home from night games. He was good at any sport he played, but never so good as at gunning and fishing. He relished competition and his abilities but never was stuck-up about them. He shared his skills with others. For instance, he coached the Dartmouth trap shooting team and me fly fishing. He and I seemed never to have trouble communicating, but wife Lillian felt it wasn't easy for him to talk with her and the children.

After graduating from high school in June 1945, the draft took Bill into the army and to the occupation forces in Germany. He rose to master sergeant, which I consider an achievement. The draft took me in August and kept me at Fort Devens. I took leave in November, to go deer hunting with Mr. DeVaux. Mrs. DeVaux no longer hunted. I think he wanted company.

Bushes and trees were turning black against early November snow when Mr. DeVaux shot a buck. A cold wind increased the incentive for getting home. We tied the thin rope he had brought along around the horns (ant-lers if you prefer) and began dragging. Although the snow allowed the deer to slide easier, the pull exhausted us. The car came into sight on the road below, down a short but steepish, brush-covered slope. I'd heard of riding a dead deer, so I got it to the brink, pushed it over and sat on it, holding the head up by the antlers to avoid obstacles. Beast and burden reached bottom after some entanglements. Mr. DeVaux and I heaved it onto the front fender and drove to the reporting station in the village. Home, after stringing him up, we went into the kitchen. I was shaking so that I had to hold my tea mug with both hands.

After the army I went to Dartmouth College and Bill became a surveyor. A few years later, he and his wife, Lil, bought land and a house on the Goodrich Four Corners road. In a remodeled shed beside the house, Bill opened his gun shop. Lil managed the household, bore Cindy, Deni, and Dave, and kept the books for the business. Winters, Bill supplemented his income by plowing driveways with his pickup. Helped by Bill's and his father's reputation as marksmen, Mister's reputation as a gunsmith, and Bill's reputation for selling only quality weapons at fair prices, the business prospered. Bill bought and sold guns, worked on rifles, sighted them in—resting them on a bench at the back of the shop and firing at targets through a small window cut for the purpose. He reloaded rifle and shotgun shells for sale and his own use, the latter with a device that reloaded a half-dozen at once. Weekly, he hosted trap shoots at a range he had marked out on a lawn beside the shop. This had five stations, around which shooters rotated, and a dog-kennel-sized house with an electric machine that threw clay pigeons on command. For a fee, individuals or teams would come and shoot—often buying shells Bill had reloaded.

Bill became a national champion at the Grand American World Trapshooting Championships held annually in August in Ohio. In 1977, he and son Deni won the national parent and child team championship breaking 396 of 400 birds. In his later years, a tremor in his hands from a powerful arthritis medicine harmed his accuracy and he shot trap less often, but he continued to be as good as ever in the field. Deni has continued the tradition. In August 2002, he won the Grand American Handicap, the most prestigious event at the championship. Firing from the biggest handicap position, the 27 yards distance behind the trap house, he broke 100 of 100 birds and then 50 of 50 in a shoot off—the first time this had been done at the Grand American.

In the years I was in college and the year I was a reporter for the *Valley News* (the local newspaper), we continued hunting and fishing together, although less often than we wished. We compensated for the lack by recalling incidents and adventures. Often this was while sitting over a cribbage board, fueled by a gallon of milk and a bushel of Oreos. We remembered driving slowly toward Beaver Meadow along a back road early one morning to go fishing. A red fox with a beautiful plume jumped in front of us from the embankment. He cantered along ahead of us for a minute or two, occasionally looking over his shoulder, apparently pleased by the opportunity to show off. Suddenly, he popped up the other embankment and disappeared.

We never stopped laughing about the time I got the Red Terror stuck, despite its 20-inch wheels. We were going 'chuck hunting and I took a farm road still soft from the spring thaw. Suddenly we were not moving; the wheels were in mud 20 inches deep. Shoveling and rocking the car to break loose failed. Into the bargain, I was in a walking cast from a skiing accident. Try jumping on a shovel to sink it into the ground wearing one useful leg. Salvation came from fence posts lying on the grass beside the road. Perhaps someone had used them to get himself out of a rut. Anyway, don't look a gift post in the mouth. We used the posts to build a corduroy road, and with Bill pushing and me exhorting we got the car to dry land. I think I have a photo of this circus somewhere.

Bill's business went from doing well to doing splendidly when he was commissioned to sell the guns from two estates. He had known these collectors for some years, and they knew his solid reputation. At one time, the racks around the shop wall held dozens of Winchesters from one collection. I think there was one rifle for each model the company had made. The mass was impressive and the guns beautiful—oiled full-length stocks of the army carbines used in the Indian wars, the gleaming barrels of the sporting guns. For the second collector, Bill sold a collection of Parker shotguns. For selling each collection, he received a 20 percent commission.

Our common pleasure in guns did not translate into agreement on government policy. He feared those who wished to have guns nationally registered. I saw no harm in it, and reminded him of our youth when we had to get permits from New Hampshire to carry handguns there on our fishing expeditions. Bill thought that enforcement of state laws—especially in Vermont—would be sufficient for gun control (an argument with merit for many localities), and he feared that registration with the federal government would make it possible for a government to disarm citizens. Although long a member of the National Rifle Association, Bill did not share the crazy conspiracy theories conjured up by its then leadership. His fear was latent, the NRA's predictive. As a boy I had been an NRA member and an avid reader of its magazine *National Rifleman* but that was when the NRA was for hunters, citizen marksmanship, and gun safety.

Different perspectives contributed to our disagreement. He had a rural perspective and I an urban one. Gun-owning in rural areas, particularly rifles and shotguns, was and is a different proposition from possession in cities and suburbs, where long guns are fewer and short guns plentiful. And the purposes of gun owning are vastly different. In cities, short gun possession is primarily for those with criminal intent or for self-defense against criminals. In rural areas possession is primarily for hunting; self-defense comes in a distant second. Forty years ago a friend of mine, consulting for the NRA, recommended that it adopt two policies on gun ownership, one for cities and one for the country. The NRA wouldn't hear of it.

To wind up a discourse that has taken me away from the DeVauxs and Bill, the advent of assault weapons—large-magazine, semi-automatic rifles and handguns—has twisted gun owning out of shape. These are not sporting weapons, but killing machines. Those who claim they need these rifles for hunting are utterly wrongheaded, if not worse. I have a Walter Mitty dream of facing an opponent in the Senate who says that his constituents need AK47s for hunting, and I reply, contemptuously, "Don't they know how to shoot?"

Our argument wasn't going anywhere, so we dropped it.

At the beginning of this piece, Bill's shop was bare of all but a few of his personal guns, either standing in the rack behind the counter or lying under the counter's glass top. My memories are racked for self-keeping. We knew he was dying. Characteristically, Bill tried to ease my burden by not seeming to be. Saying goodbye, which I don't think we did, wasn't easy. I just drove away. He was buried, after a funeral ceremony he had designed himself, at the top of Hillside Cemetery. There was a beautiful view from the grave. Bill would have enjoyed it.

My farewell to Millie DeVaux—Charlie having died earlier—was less tearing but more oppressive. I knocked at the screen door to the familiar kitchen and went on into the next room. She was collapsed like a sack into a chair in the middle of a bare room. A breeze moved the gauze curtains in the windows out to the front porch. The picture had the tensions of a Wyeth painting. When she recognized my voice, she roused, and a few minutes talk brought back echoes of its once boisterous heartiness. I could see her in the kitchen stirring a pot and leading the sallies against someone present. But soon she lapsed into quietness. I did not need to tiptoe from the room. I doubt she heard me go.

CHAPTER FOURTEEN

A Skiing Memoir

For us youngsters in Norwich, ski season began long before snow fell.

Months of longing began with the signs of autumn. The road home from school was baked almost white from August heat. Goldenrod bowed by its edges, the asters paled, the spikes of mallow withered. Corn stubble pierced the brown fields. Only pastures and grass for the rowen continued green. On the common after school, football replaced baseball.

We enjoyed, and we knew winter was coming.

October: Frosts whitened the fields in the morning; we made green tracks as we crossed them. The hills glowed with the maples orange and red and the yellow from the beeches, made all the more vivid by interspersed patches of black-green pines. My mother had lined shelves in a cellar room with produce from our large garden: Mason jars of peas, beans, yellow squash, tomatoes, and corn. A screened cupboard held tumblers of her wild grape and apple-currant jellies. In the front cellar with its dirt floor, parsnips and carrots hibernated in troughs of sand. On heavy wire racks Hubbard squash, dark green and big as boulders, began to harden. By Thanksgiving and Christmas we had to axe them into pieces to be boiled to scoop out the orange meat. We were snug with the sense of harvest done. This ache to tuck-in come fall has never left me.

We knew winter was coming.

November grew colder. The ground froze. Ice skimmed ponds. We studied the semaphore arms of leafless trees and sniffed the air like hounds for signals of snow. Clouds and tree trunks were the best predictors. Slate-colored or black clouds meant rain—gloomy rain—as did tree trunks black in evening light. A soft gray sky the color of beech trunks meant it might snow. Our anticipation grew.

We knew winter was coming.

On a day in December, as unpredictable as the flocking of crows, we were moved to begin preparations.

Father had established a carpenter shop between the woodshed—with its racks of two-foot, split maple for the fireplace—and the garage. Here, along one wall, was a heavy, scarred workbench with a long, wooden two-handled vice fixed to its side. There were hooks and racks for tools. Across from the bench stood a woodstove converted to kerosene by inserting burners with circular wicks between vertical metal cylinders. The wicks were fed kerosene through a copper tube from a glass jug like those used today in office water coolers. We refilled this from a spigot in a 75-gallon drum in the garage. The jug gurgled when the fire drank.

Intent as priests, and fully as devout, we began our ritual. Into the shop from the attic we brought the icons stored there since spring. We took off the stretchers used to keep the ski tips from losing their curve. We undid the clamps just before the tips and at the heels, releasing the wooden block placed between their centers to preserve their camber—a slight concave curve in each ski. For these were flat wooden skis; if they had lost their camber over the summer the front of the ski wouldn't bite into the snow, making both control and turning especially difficult. No one then imagined skis that would keep their camber—or with steel edges. Later, even ridge-topped wood skis, although stiffer, demanded this care.

After screwing the vice to hold the ski tight, we sanded the top and applied varnish to cover last year's scarring so as to keep out this year's damp. The bottom was most important. With pieces of metal and shards of glass saved from broken window panes, we scraped it clean and sanded it smooth. A tin of pine tar from the hardware store warming on the stove filled the shop with a scent divine. Had we had the imagination, we would have believed that we were burning incense to the snow gods. But we were content to be intoxicated by the aroma and our devotions. For me, still, no perfume can compare.

We brushed on the pine tar and burned it into the wood with a blowtorch, wiping off the excess before applying other coats and burning them in. Completely incensed, we stood that ski against the wall, on its tip to preserve the curve, and turned to the other. Skis so prepared slid well on damp snow, and they held the wax needed for dry snow. Without this waterproofing, the bare bottom absorbed water, snow stuck to it, sliding was reduced to leaden plodding. The all-conditions bottoms on today's skis would have seemed miraculous to us. No bottom preparation or wax worked in great cold. One morning when the thermometer registered 40 degrees below zero, our skis wouldn't slide. When it warmed up to 25 below, we could go skiing.

With the bottoms finished, we turned to our harnesses—"bindings" then not being in our vocabulary. Their parts began with toe irons—a metal plate screwed to the ski with sides imprisoning the boot toe to keep the boot aligned with the ski. A leather strap threaded through a slot in the irons kept the boot toe from popping up. Metal hooks fastened thick leather straps to the outsides of the toe irons. The straps went around the heel of the boot; a toggle buckle tightened them. We greased the leather to keep it supple.

In the years before toe irons, boots were held (so to speak) to the skis by a strap over the boot toe. This "toe strap" had been threaded through a slot in the ski. No strap controlled the boot heel. Too often boots and skis took separate directions

Our heels were not held tight to the ski, which made turning harder and walking and climbing much easier. For us, these harnesses were the latest thing, but the principles

behind them dated from the 1890s, and their close ances-
tor had been used by Captain Robert Scott of England and
Roauld Amundson, a Norwegian, on their Antarctic expe-
dition in 1911-1912. Amundson discovered the South Pole.
In the 1920s, Marius Eriksen had manufactured a harness
like ours. He also had for long been Norway's most famous
ski maker. Marius's son, Stein, who won the giant slalom
gold in the Oslo Olympics in 1952, now has a lodge in Park
City, Utah. Our devotions made our Saturdays blissful.

We knew winter was coming.

On a day snow would come. Perhaps the raw air and the
gray light would foretell the coming snow. In the afternoon
the air whitened as small flakes drifted down, tentative,
uncertain whether to stay and where to rest. The latter
depended on the ground being frozen. We followed the
course of each flake, fearing there might not be another.
Oblivious to their geometry, we monitored their fate. It's
sticking, we'd screech. But not until the bare earth was
white and only spears of grass stuck up did anxiety ebb and
confidence grow that this might be the real thing. Then
we'd retire to the fireplace and drink hot cocoa, rich with
a dash of vanilla extract.

Perhaps the snow would come at night, after a soft gray
evening. My bedroom window looked down the pasture,
over the meadows by Blood Brook, and up the fields to the
road between Norwich and Hanover, New Hampshire.
I would wake up in the night and look to see if the car
lights on the road shone fuzzy. This meant snow. And if

the steam-train whistle was clear for Lewiston depot in the Connecticut River valley between Norwich and Hanover, it meant an easterly wind and a promising storm. I curled under the feather puff, suspended between the ecstasy of it snowing and the agony that it might stop.

We greeted the day with "How much?" Anything over five inches, even if some hay stubble remained uncovered, brought out skis and bamboo poles, which in those days came with large webbed rings for soft snow. Dressed in corduroy pants, leather ski boots, sweaters, and knitted hats, we buckled our harnesses and set out single file over intervening slopes for the big hill. We ducked through a barbwire fence and across barely covered needles under a grove of pines, taking turns breaking track. The air bit noses and cheeks and tasted good. The clear cold and slanting sun made our track shadows blue. We knew then that they were true, those stories about Paul Bunyan and the winter of the blue snows.

Sliding easily, because our heels came off the skis, and sidestepping or herringboning or traversing up the hills (using the kickturn we had learned), we came panting to our destination. The big hill doesn't look so big now, nor so steep. But from the top of it, in the morning, we looked upon a world gentled by snow. Then we began the hard work of breaking out the slope, sidestepping down and up and down and up again. We needed a packed area because we hadn't learned to ski in deep snow. Climbing and packing strengthened our legs and taught us more about

maneuvering our long skis than we would have from riding
a lift up and coming down on machine packed snow. Skis
became natural extensions of our feet.

We knew the joy, the reward, of descent from the
effort of ascent—a lifting of the heart that we later felt
on mountain snowfields that we climbed with sealskins on
our skis and rucksacks on our backs. Sealskins were just
that: made of sealskin, ski-width wide, hooked by a loop
to the toe of the ski. The hair faced backwards, preventing
the ski from slipping backwards while allowing a forward
slide. There was a later substitute made from plush that
helped when climbing but did not slide. I still have a pair
of skins, stored with mothballs, somewhere in a shoebox.

Hannes Schneider, who came to New England from
Austria about 1939, became the acknowledged father of
the Austrian Arlberg technique in the United States—
and a popular parent-hero he was. Yet he was more the
grandfather here, for although he had originated the technique at St. Anton, in Austria, it had been brought here
nearly a decade earlier by other Austrians who became ski
instructors at the big resorts like North Conway, Cannon
Mountain, Mount Mansfield, and Yosemite—where, if
skillful, some married heiresses.

We picked up this technique as best we could. We
hadn't heard of St. Anton, and Arlberg may have been
the first foreign word we learned. The snowplow was our
emergency brake—heels of our skis as far apart as possible,
ski tips together, legs braced. The stem was similar to the

snowplow, but less extreme. The stem was the basic posi-
tion/building block for the Arlberg technique, beginning
with the stem turn. If we were going straight down the
hill, we took a modified stem position and then weighted
one ski, bent that knee slightly forward, and rotated our
body in the direction of the ski tip, and in that direction
we would go!

If we were traversing the hill, we did much the same,
except that we began the turn by "winding up" (rotating
our shoulders up the hill), accompanying this with bending the knee of the downhill leg, and then pushing off this
leg as we simultaneously rotated our chests down the hill.
If the skis obeyed, we pointed down the hill. We completed the turn by rotating in the direction from which
we came. Our weight should have been predominantly on
the inside edge of the downhill ski when we were traversing and then winding up and as we finished the turn. This
up and down while winding up and rotating the shoulders
provided the power for getting the skis from the traverse
to the fall line (pointing downhill) and across it to traverse the other direction.

At first, this didn't come easy. Falling often, we had
much practice in getting up, lying on our backs and
swinging our skis over until they were below us, parallel
to the hill. We called the long indentations we made in
the snow bathtubs. Going too fast, our instinctive reaction was to lean back to stop. It works, if you don't mind
using your butt for a brake. The result was sitzmarks.

Later, for a time, I wrote a column in a local newspaper entitled *Linked Sitzmarks*.

We also tried getting around using the jump turn, which meant putting both poles beside your boots below you and jumping around to face the other way—a sort of 180-degree pole vault. This was clumsy and unusable at any speed. Then there was the step turn, diagrammed seriously in how-to-ski books with black and white skis stepping around—rather like teaching a baby to walk by painting black and white footprints on the floor. Both testify to the primitive—at least the unsophisticated—state of technique at the time. We also tried the open *christie*, which we executed by leaning back a bit and putting weight on the outside edge of our uphill ski. This nonsensical procedure came and went as impractical, for it only turned us into the hill and caused frequent spills when the heels of our skis crossed. In soft snow, some of us tried the *telemark* (from Norway's Telemark district) with limited success: it demanded very good balance.

We would leave the big hill at dusk. Sore legged and cold, noses dripping, frustrated and fulfilled, we went home on our outgoing track. And so it went, never stale: days, weeks, months, winters.

At other times, we toured through the woods on old logging roads or around trees, dodging branches. On a windless day, the woods were quiet as quiet. Silent doesn't work here for the word has a sibilant sound, whether spoken or in your head. The "st" in still is too noisy;

hushed is equally so. Even quiet has that sharp "t" at the end. (Does anyone know a satisfactory word?) Standing among the soft grays of sapling trunks and the contrasting green-black of young hemlocks, looking for rabbit, fox, or partridge tracks, sound absent, we could hear our hair grow. Time and space combined. Comfort settled over us. Then a chickadee might call or a whiff of breeze rattle unshed beech leaves.

If it was snowing large flakes, the quiet was even thicker; hard flakes of dry powder hissed as they brushed the beech leaves. If with a companion, we didn't talk, or only briefly in low voices. Nothing said could equal the value of saying nothing. What had been a stack of wood made humps in the snow. Once it had been a cord (four foot lengths, four feet high, and eight feet long) held between bookends of trees. Now the remnants were engaged in what Robert Frost called the "slow, smokeless burning of decay." This was where a farmer had cut his stove wood or a woodcutter had made his five dollars—the fee, before chain saws, for a cord cut and stacked in the woods.

At age 40, my father bought skis and joined us. In a perpetual stem, he smiled tolerantly when we called, Hurry up. He bushwhacked a narrow trail through the steep ravine up from Will Bond's field to Mary Williams's field at the top of the hill. Pines lined the ravine's slopes, and where they met Mary's field there was a big bittersweet vine, remnants of its red and orange berries like lanterns against both pine and snow. On an early map of the secret places in my domain, I had marked the vine with a special symbol. With snow enough we could sidestep up Will's field, through the ravine, and into the top field. Coming down, we got up enough speed at the top to make turning into the ravine chancy. Relieved to have made it, we still had to stem like hell to stay out of the trees. Emerging in Will's field, we relished our escape and let the skis run as fast as we dared, our eyes watering from the wind.

Many of the innovations in equipment that came along during the Thirties helped to improve our skiing. Steel edges greatly increased our control. Bindings that held boot heels tighter to the ski equally increased control and brought us to more advanced Arlberg technique. We learned the *stem christie*, much like the stem turn, but the skis came together, parallel, as you finished the turn. More advanced was the *christie*—or *christiana*—turn with the skis remaining parallel. The principles of up-down, windup, and rotation were constants. Bending the knees forward and downward—NOT as though sitting in a chair—was essential to skiing Arlberg, or most any technique in any era. With boot heels still coming up off the ski, this was difficult. But how to fasten them down? Various devices were tried. The French developed the long-thong binding, using a metal toe plate and with a long leather strap threaded though a slot in the ski and wrapped around the ankle. A few individuals tried screwing the boot to the ski—a short-lived experiment.

In the mid-Thirties, the Bildstein spring came along—a coiled spring about six inches long fastened with a strap around the ankle and hooked to the ski behind the heel. We bought and used these once we could afford them. But earlier we had a homemade device. We cut automobile tire inner tubes into rings, put two of them together with metal split rings, and strapped one end around our ankles and hooked the other to the ski. These didn't hold our heels down really tight, but they were a big help. And we could unhook them from the ski when climbing or touring on the flat.

Much better was the Kandahar cable binding, invented in 1932. This had a toeplate with longer sides and lugs, instead of a toestrap, to hold the boot toe down. The cable around the boot heel held it in the toe plate when tightened by a throw screwed to the ski in front of the boot. Guides screwed to the side of the ski pulled the cable down and the heel with it. For a time, toeplates were made with cable guides on the sides, and when the cable was run through these the heel could rise slightly from the ski. Harnesses and Kandahar bindings were straightforward and simple. With a little instruction, anyone could mount them on the ski, and I spent hours working in a ski shop doing so. The modern safety binding, although safer, is mechanical wizardry, sold, mounted, and adjusted by professionals at the cost of hundreds of dollars.

Cross-country tourers and racers used a different ski, lighter and narrower. Today's racing cross-country skis are even narrower. I bought a pair of hickory cross-country skis from Art Bennett's shop in Hanover in the late Forties. But I began to tour seriously only when I lived in Norway in the Fifties. The bindings were Dovre, Bergendahl, and Rottefella. The latter, colloquially called rat-trap, had vertical pins in the toeplate that fitted into holes drilled in the very front of the boot sole. A front throw held the boot tightly down on the pins. The boot heel could come fully off the ski, so that the technique was somewhat like running. Many still call the sport langlauf, or longrun.

For us, steel edges were the equivalent of going to the moon, because the edges of our skis had become so rounded with wear that they skidded when turning on packed snow. We were like a hog on ice in worse conditions. Although Lettner steel edges for the bottom of the ski had been patented in 1928, we did not have them. And we learned only later that Marius Eriksen had patented a steel edge screwed to the side of the ski about the same time. In the early days, skis did not come with steel edges attached. Craftsmen in ski shops routed the edges of the ski and screwed on the edges. These were made in lengths of maybe ten inches and proved vulnerable to the rocks, stumps, and other hazards of New England conditions. I spent many hours in the cellar of the Dartmouth Co-op repairing them. Today, because they are built into skis at the factory, edges are very strong.

A few years after we began skiing, hickory—we called it hickry—replaced the ash of our early skis, as ash had replaced pine and birch. Ridgetops replaced flat skis, for they were stiffer and bit into the snow better. Gregg, Northland, and Groswold were the common brands. We could not afford the better Norwegian skis made by Marius Eriksen or the laminated Splitkein, or Hovde or the Swiss ski, Attenhofer. We kept using our Tonkin (bamboo) ski poles. They were stronger and safer than the new aluminum or the later steel poles, which could break like a stick. If you broke a bamboo pole, it splintered and did not become pieces with lethal ends. Early first aid instructions for skiing accidents described how to treat a stomach pierced by a steel or aluminum pole: "leave it in, immobilize it, and go like hell for the doctor."

Boot designs and manufacturers proliferated. The new cable bindings so compressed the soles of boots, fore and aft, that a steel shank had to be introduced to prevent them from buckling into the arch of the foot. Magic potions, made to protect the bottoms of skis and to hold wax, filled fancy tins and bottles. Waxes for various snow conditions appeared. Daubed on and smoothed out with applied heat or the palm of the hand, they made a big difference. If you chose the right wax, well and good; if you didn't, you might as well have applied glue. Waxes, especially for touring or cross-country racing, were designed to provide both glide and enough stick under the foot to give traction for the next glide and for climbing hills.

Corduroy pants gave way to gabardine ski pants, tapered, with an elastic to go under the foot to hold them inside the boot. Socks went inside pants so as not to gather snow. Sweaters and windbreakers, which we called parkas, kept the rest of us warm. Many pleasure skiers and racers traded knickerbockers and knee socks for ski pants. For the fashion conscious and the after-ski crowd, there were stores like Andre's of New York. It advertised trousers designed by the city's finest custom tailors and "tested on the trails." They were said to fit snugly at the waist and hips and taper in a tightly-drawn modern silhouette. Andre's claimed that their leather boots were handmade on a correct orthopedic last. An Andre's outfit—hickory skis with a silver-lac-quered running surface, cable bindings, steel poles (plain or colored)—was priced (1942) at $19.95. Grand though this ensemble was, it was sober, even stylish, compared with modern skiers' neon wardrobe and moon boots. (The boots, I regret having to admit, do increase one's control of the skis.) In our dress, we slowly adopted ski pants; other-wise we were seedily content.

Our world widened. With some increase in skill from age, father's willingness occasionally to transport us fur-ther afield, and the appearance of the rope tow, we spent more time going down bigger hills. These early tows were powered by old cars or farm tractors. To carry the weight of the rope and a load of passengers, they had to operate at a constant, fairly good speed. To grab this fast-moving rope firmly was to be shamed: jerked face first into the snow before the pitying multitude. Into the bargain you got burned if you fell so that the rope ran over you. So, with heavy leather mittens, preferably reinforced across the palm, you grasped the rope loosely, picking up speed gradually until it was safe to hang on tight. On long rides or when the rope went over a hump in the hill, its weight lengthened arms and destroyed shoulders. The temptation was to rest it on your hipbone. But the rope rolled and your parka might roll with it. At the top of the hill you might find that you and the rope had become joined at the hip, headed for the return wheel. After a few beheadings and amputations, tow operators arranged a barrier, which if broken stopped the rope.

In Woodstock, we skied at Gilbert's, named after the farmer whose land it was. A metal roadside plaque now memorializes Gilbert's as, in 1934, the first rope tow in New England. Then came Bunny's Suicide Six, a steep slope that then only the brave could take straight—in part because there was limited space at the bottom to stop. Today's downhill racers would think it a mild schuss. Closer to home was Cemetery Hill in Norwich—so called for the town's graveyard nearby, where, contrary to myth, a couple of graves were not kept open in winter for luckless skiers. This was the cemetery to which, when much younger, we marched on Memorial Day. Then there came the J-bar at Oak Hill in Hanover and the T-bar—the more romantic he-she stick. Older, we ventured far afield to Cannon Mountain, Mt. Mansfield, and Janet Mead's Pico Peak—where we met young Andrea Mead and admired the tailoring of her mother's ski pants.

Many of us sensed a mission to pass our joys on to others, along with such technique as we possessed. Besides, teaching was great fun. Ford and Peggy Sayre managed the Hanover Inn and started its ski school at Christmas for city youngsters, ages maybe six to ten. They bunked on the top floor of the inn, storied for its pillow fights and the kid who one night tossed his artificial leg under his bunk, proclaiming that it was the only leg in the room that wasn't tired. We youngsters, female and male, a half-dozen years older than they, skied with them every day, teaching them basics—sidestep, herringbone, snowplows, and stem turns. We took them touring, which would have been short hikes had they been on foot. Many were the dusks we coaxed weary bodies off the snow and the final hundred yards to the road and a ride back to the inn.

In January, midmonth, the thaw that bore its name would come—a week of dread that winter might be over. But cold would return, sometimes making it too icy or crusty to ski. Try crust skiing without steel edges. Then we would go sliding on the road down our hill—until official-dom sanded it. We tobogganed on the hills, both daytime and with moonlight gleaming on the crust. But the crust had to be thick and solid. Otherwise it broke, trapping your boots and making it miserable to tow the toboggan back up the hill. Wild were those rides. Thinking of snow conditions reminds me: In those days Vermont and New Hampshire ski areas reported their snow conditions to the Boston Globe using a number code. One evening, a bit out of focus, our reporter coded wet, drifting, crust.

By the end of February, skiing paled even for us. For a couple of weeks, skis cooled in the woodshed. We greased our boots and set them by the stove, the better to absorb the grease. As the sun rose higher, the snow melted during the day and froze at night, making corn snow—an inch or two of snow-ice granules on top of the winter's well-settled base. This near-perfect skiing renewed our enthusiasm, and we returned to the slopes.

We learned that giants walked the snow in Hanover across the river—veritable Odins—whether skiing cross country, downhill, slalom, or jumping. Had their names been writ in gold, they could not have shone brighter for us: Chivers, Bradley, Meservy, Hannah, Durrance, Hunter, Washburn, Proctor, Litchfield, Woods, Wells, McLane. Four Dartmouth skiers went to the 1936 Olympics. Nine would have gone to the 1940 Olympics, had they been held. The philosophy of Otto Schniebs, the Dartmouth coach during the first half of the Thirties, became our own: skiing is not a sport, it is a way of life. Then came Walter Prager, a Swiss and a champion in his own country in cross-country and downhill racing—four-time winner of the Arlberg Kandahar downhill race. Walter once said that he came to Hanover with "Jesus Christ and apple pie a la mode" as his only English, startling his hostess, Mrs. Chivers, mother of the famous Chivers sons. Once, after the McGill Winter Carnival in Montreal, Charley Proctor, head of the Dartmouth Outing Club and later a fixture at

Yosemite, called Prager into the office and accused, "I've heard you waxed the McGill team's cross-country skis at its Carnival." Walter replied that he had because they needed help. "Best thing you ever did," said Proctor.

We worshipped these greats from afar, and up close if there was opportunity, endeavoring to ski as they did. We rejoiced in ski lore and sang their songs: "We're from the Arlberg Ski School/An honorable clan are we/We'll teach you to ski for a dollar/For a dollar we'll teach you to ski." And to the tune of the *Whiffenpoof Song*: "So it's doctors and lawyers and students we/Ski, ski, ski," etc. And: "Two boards upon cold powder snow, yo-ho/The craziest song that I know/Two boards upon cold powder snow, yo-ho/ What more does a man need to know?" We sang also in Norwegian and German without understanding either.

A few years earlier, another giant had entered my life. He became a close friend, a mentor for me in skiing, and an example for life.

I first saw Marshall Fitzgerald in a tree. We had a huge rock maple at the end of our driveway. The trunk at the butt must have been six feet through, the lower limbs thicker than nail kegs. Father thought these might tear off in a storm, although obviously they had survived many. Also, there was rot in some places. To do the needful, he hired two men at Dartmouth who worked on trees. Marsh was one of them.

Provided this small boy kept a safe distance, he was allowed to watch. The work began with setting the safety ropes. Marsh and the other man each made a bundle of one end of his rope and twirled it so it flew over a lower limb; they then flipped it until the bundle descended on the other side, doubling the rope. Grabbing this, they walked up the trunk—no ladders—and repeated the process until the rope was set around a high limb. With a bowline-on-a-bight, each made a seat and tied the tag end of that line around the standing rope. Marsh called that knot four half-hitches, two each way. When I started rock climbing, I found that the learned term is a prussic knot. The marvel of it is that the stress on the knot from the weight of a man sitting in the bowline-seat causes the knot to divide so it will not slide on the standing rope. Marsh thus had a secure seat leaving his hands free for work. To complete the marvel, when the sitter wants to descend, he squeezes the half-hitches together so that they will slide on the standing rope. Try it with half-inch rope. It works.

Marsh's skill at this entranced me. Wanting to go to a limb in front of and below him, he swung out, squeezed the knot, and slid down the standing rope to that limb, landing like a great bird. I learned that his grace in that maple characterized his skiing and much that he did in life. To return to the tree, Marsh and the other man (for the record, Gordon Cloud) cut out the weak and rotten wood with gouges and wooden mallets and filled the wounds with special cement. They secured the heaviest limbs to higher limbs with guy wires, and trimmed out other limbs with hand saws, daubing the scars with tar.

My young boy's admiration for Marsh must have been a trial for him. When I pleaded to be taken fishing, he took me plug-casting for bass on Lake Morey. In the winter when he repaired skis and steel edges in the basement of the Dartmouth Co-op, he let me hang around and taught me how to do what he was doing. When he married a nurse from Hanover hospital, Elisabeth, as lovely as he was handsome and fit, they took me skiing. Both were certified ski instructors. In the late Thirties, they went to Yosemite National Park for a couple of years to teach in Luggi Foeger's ski school. By this time, we had become friends.

Pearl Harbor and the declaration of war immediately made Marsh decide to join the Air Force. Awaiting enlistment, he went to Dartmouth's Baker Library to study everything he could about aeronautics, aircraft, and flying. In flight school, he distinguished himself, among other ways, by taking some ten seconds off the obstacle course record.

This studying and inquiring marked Marsh's life. He had not been to college, but he had that marvelous contraption, the mind of the Yankee tinker. He examined the surface of things and pondered their inner workings, the why and the how. I remember his wonder at the lift of an airplane's wing and his immediate effort to discover why. He would use a tool, think how to improve it, and often make it better. He would pick up a device, turn it over in his hands, peer at it, set it back on the work bench. The cheer on his face would settle into soberness. He'd pick it up again and peer at it, all the while wondering how to use it in new ways or how to make it work better. The shape his hands and fingers assumed when studying an object were as though he were sculpting it. I recall some of the times when his innovations improved the manufacturing processes and products of his employers—for which he got little credit. He had a mind for inner principles. This must have come from father Ernest, who, later in his life, became the general custodian of the scientific equipment in Dartmouth's physics laboratory. The department's chairman, Professor Meservy, thought him more competent and intelligent than some of the professors there.

Marsh applied his analytical bent to skiing. He loved the sport and shared his insights. He kept me under his wing as he did many other youngsters, male and female. When teaching Arlberg technique in the Thirties, he explained more clearly than other instructors the proper way to shift weight when turning. Watching a pupil fall or have trouble making those boards do his bidding, he always looked several stages back, seeking the cause behind the cause behind the immediate difficulty. This was not the old refrain of "bend zee knees, five dollars please."

Returning to skiing and teaching in Aspen after the war, he discovered, it seems to me, the principle that lies behind modern turning, whether pleasure skiing or slalom racing: the body above the waist, particularly the shoulders, should not drive the turn—as it did skiing Arlberg style. The hips and legs should move from side to side like a pendulum (the hips NOT rotating), the knees and the ski's edges causing the skis to turn. The upper body's weight and forward lean reinforced the turn. The first great practitioner of this style, in my view, was Stein Eriksen during the 1952 Olympics at Oslo, where he won a gold and a silver medal. Andrea Mead Lawrence won two golds at Oslo, while skiing closer to Arlberg. I had the privilege of watching these two races thanks to a minor job with the Norwegian Olympic Committee.

Soon after he first wears skis, every boy, and many a girl, builds a jump. It seems as inevitable as lacing boots. Initially, the jump made of snow will be a foot high, and the distance travelled in the air, if any, will be a few feet— maybe soon followed by a bathtub. As the jumps grow bigger, the airborne distance may reach ten to twenty feet. Because the whole operation is on the even slope of the hill, jumping farther means being higher off the ground during flight and coming back to snow correspondingly harder. Somehow, we learned that if a jump was set back from a knoll, we could go longer distances while getting little higher off the ground than we were when passing over the knoll. We learned the nomenclature—the inrun, coming down to the lip, or takeoff—of the jump; the knoll; the landing (hill); and the transition, from the landing to the outrun (level where we could stop). The steeper the landing, within reason, the softer we returned to snow because gravity, as well as our speed, pushed us down the hill instead of into the ground.

For years, jumping gave me great trouble. Despite constant practice it eluded me. In the air I was OK, but I couldn't hold my landing. I fell and fell again. This was partly because I had not learned a telemark landing—one foot ahead of the other—to keep from pitching forward, and the deeply bent rear knee pushing the other foot back to provide a prop against falling backward. Landing as though sitting in a chair is very unsteady and, in competition, costs style points. All through grade school I was a dud. In high school I competed only in slalom, winning once.

We jumped using our everyday skis, but in college I graduated to jumpers. Jumping skis in those days were heavy hickory (today they're plastic), about four inches wide, with three grooves to help the ski track straight (instead of the downhill ski's one groove), and typically were eight feet long. We used Kandahar cable bindings. We, and even the top jumpers, adjusted the bindings to hold our heels down on the skis. This long-persisting error prevented jumpers from having enough forward lean to fly the great distances of competitors today. Jumpers have to lean far forward while airborne to keep the wind from pushing them onto their backs. And the greater the lean, the more the jumper rides the air to go farther down the hill. Because ankles flex only so far forward, tightly fastened heels meant that legs rose almost straight from the skis and the lean mostly came from a sharp bend at the waist. Arms were held forward. This aerodynamically unsound style characterized many European jumpers as well as Americans until nearly 1950. The Norwegians, the best performers of the era, understood this before the rest of us. They began to let their heels rise from the skis to permit more forward lean for the entire body, which, in turn, allowed them to ride the air more gracefully for longer jumps. A formula combining distance covered and points for style (20 points for perfection) produces the total score.

These days, as television watchers have noticed, jumpers lie out almost parallel above their skis, which are held in a V position to increase the sail to catch the wind. To my mind this is not so graceful as the pre-ski-flying style. Today, on the huge jump hills, skiers may fly 400 to 600 hundred feet, and distance seems more important than style. In our day, 230 feet was a more or less standard big hill and 300 feet a really BIG hill. The record jump in the United States in 1941 was 288 feet, made by the Norwegian-American Torger Tokle. Contrary to popular opinion, jumping is a safe sport: competition takes place in carefully controlled conditions, not as in downhill races where competitors may bash into trees and orange net fences.

As a freshman at Dartmouth, I resolved to make the ski team as a jumper, despite the great trouble that landing gave me for so many years. I acquired a telemark landing by imitating it in our living room dozens of times daily until it became automatic—and then at the top of the hill before each jump. Marsh coached me on the jump hill, and we spent many evenings diagramming various positions in flight seeking the best aerodynamic one. From this and from studying photos of the best Norwegian jumpers (and watching Norwegian exchange student Christian Moen, then Dartmouth's nemesis at Middlebury College, who placed second at the Holmenkollen championships in 1952), we decided that bindings allowing the boot heel to come up from the ski permitted the body to curve smoothly forward. Marsh and I also had resident models. On the Dartmouth team were my Osloian roommates, Per Jan Ranhoff and Tor Arneberg. Tor was a fine four-event skier and jumper. He helped me and I watched him.

I jumped and jumped until I could produce a creditable performance. Persistence was all, plus Marsh's coaching. I believe that intensely practicing a sport and intensely studying its techniques combine into an intellectual discipline as worthy as any other. No matter the weariness and the disgust at failures, we kept practicing. The adrenalin always flowed, pumped by the prospect of mechanically-unassisted flight, the sensation of speed, the concentration needed to jump when our feet were exactly at the edge of the takeoff, and the thrill of being airborne. I made the team, but I never jumped as well as I wished.

At Dartmouth we began each season on a small jump, proceeded to the medium-sized one among the pines in the Vale of Tempe, and then to the 40-meter jumping hill at the edge of the golf course. The twinges of anxiety that accompanied the early jumps each season on the bigger hill waned with practice, but yellow holes in the snow at the top of the inrun spoke of its vestiges. The bigger hill's landing was graded into a ravine; the inrun was a steel trestle with a plank incline with cleats to hold the snow. Walter Prager, Marsh, and I scraped and painted the trestle one summer. Already a rock climber, I learned that exposure on a cliff is far less intimidating than standing on a two-inch steel beam surrounded by a sphere of air. We roped up for the first week. Philistines in the college's administration have torn down the trestle, justifying their heresy by claiming that it was an insurance liability.

My earliest excursion to the big hill, as I recall, was in the mid-Thirties to watch the Norwegian Ruud brothers, Sigmund and Birger, perform exhibition jumps at the Dartmouth Carnival. Then they were the best there was. They soared effortlessly all the way down to the transition, and even executed a double jump, which was fashionable for a few years. I was captivated. Another part of that memorable day was that my mother—who was not an outdoorswoman and who hated wearing trousers—got her ski pants on backwards.

In 1950, when I was a senior in college, on one of those days in March when the sun is bright and the corn snow perfect, Marsh, Lib (Elizabeth), and I sought out a hill field near Norwich—rounded, south-facing, long and open. We skied and climbed and skied while their elkhound, Naki, guarded our rucksacks. We ate sandwiches sitting on our skis and drank juice cooled in the snow. We overlooked a scene peaceful and slushy, distant cows in muddy barnyards warming their backs in the sun, ruts in roads between awkward fence posts, a tin roof shining. Behind us, crowning the hill, portly elders with sap buckets gleaming as watch fobs, gave transfusions for our waffles. Smoke rose from the sugar house around the hill.

Bliss it was that day to be alive—and skiing.

I still ski, not often enough, and it excites and soothes me as much as ever—although I think that the congeniality among skiers and the reverence for the sport is far from when I became a convert.

I have lost Marsh. He died not long ago after sitting in a home far from Norwich and his house on the Maine coast. He lived in a world I could not enter and he could not leave. I hope there is skiing there. His photograph hangs on my wall.

CHAPTER FIFTEEN

BEING LEARND

An old saw says that a man who chops his own wood warms himself twice. These retrievings have warmed me twice, reliving the memories and writing them down. As I review them, I see that I put on rose-colored spectacles when very young. A small voice whispers that the town couldn't have been such a wonderful place to be raised. Then I count the wonders and decide that my accounts of them and the tint remain accurate—with minimal excursions into fantasy.

This collection began some years ago as a piece about Will Bond, gathered dust for a time, and then grew as fancy moved me. The individuals and occasions came in and out as I retrieved them with their contexts—floral, faunal, and delightful.

The tales never were contemplated as a series. Readers who demand that writing contain information of great import, or cause profound thoughts to germinate in readers' minds, surely have been disappointed.

Nevertheless, life in Norwich *learnd* me much that long has been useful. Learnd is a word manufactured for this occasion to distinguish it from the Englishism, "learnt" and from "learn<u>ed</u>," which I certainly was not. "Learnd" is not to be confused with "taught." Miz Cross was right: our teachers taught (and very well, too); they didn't "learn" us. Learning was our job. Of course, Norwich air and those breathing it taught me, but I think they learnd me more than they taught.

Although it may be narrow, the distinction is important. To be learnd is to learn from participating—a process characterized by absorption, which combines immediate experience with on-site instruction. It may come simply from observation, from something like osmosis, whose chief characteristic is absorption. The stuff that a person has been learnd is integrated with his fiber. It sinks in more than teaching typically does, because teaching hands down knowledge in individual doses. Becoming learnd cannot be taught, but its virtues may be preached. Being learnd bears a resemblance to imprinting among animals and birds, a source of its longevity.

To be a farmer in Norwich was to be learnd by confrontation with life's essentials, like the milk check. When I was a youngster farmers with cows put their milk in 45 quart cans and set them on a platform where the farm road joined the town road. The creamery truck would pick up the milk, weigh it, and the farmer would get his milk check at the end of the month—cash essential for meeting grain bills.

A farmer, one especially strapped this month, took his check to the bank, passed it through the wicket, and was handed money. This he counted, counted several more times, and counted again. The line behind him grew longer, feet shuffled, and impatience became audible. The cashier said to him, "Ain't it all theyah?"

"Jest barely," he answered.

Will Bond learnd me more than how to carry a pig. He learnd me stoicism when he, without complaint, sold off most of his farm to pay heavy medical bills. Townspeoples' conduct of affairs in the fire company, on the school board, in town meeting, on the street, learnd me civility, patience, acceptance of the other fellow—if his warts weren't too big. Norwichers were not taught to govern themselves effectively. They learnd themselves—even if the resulting harmony was imperfect. Their conduct learnd me. Norwich claimed no intellectual property rights to the prescription that produced such an environment. Citizens thought well of their town, but they were not given to self-congratulation. They would have understood my mother's oft repeated maxim, "Pride goeth before a fall."

Jack Cray learnd me to look behind assertions of any kind. Are the facts of the situation as they're asserted to be? Are promises to be taken as made? He did this by asking a fellow who had praised his own ability, "Let's see you shoot." Nowhere, in my experience abroad and at home, is that truer than in political and intelligence analysis or when buying a horse. A man went into a sales stable and inspected a gelding praised by the liveryman. "Take the halter off him and let him walk around." Freed, the horse took three steps and bumped smack into a post. "Damn you for trying to sell me a blind horse."

"Blind, hell," explained the liveryman. "He just don't give a damn."

The caution is even more apt given the information glut—so often marked by fabrication and deception—that dominates American public life. *Vermont Is Where You Find It*, a photo book published some years ago, shows two men in overalls standing at the rear of a group listening to a stump speaker. "What's he talkin' about?" one asks. Replies the other, "He don't say."

Miz Cross, in our conversation, wondered why she had talked so much about her mother and father. They were just "ordinary people," she said. Yes, were we all so ordinary. Her father, farmer/road commissioner; mother, teacher in school and in the kitchen; both readers, players in village theatricals, and ponderers of religious truths; members of an extended family who bestowed great care on one another. She learnd me again about the worth of ordinary people, whether in Johnson or Union Village or Norwich—perhaps even elsewhere. Knowing who she was, she educated Norwichers' children excellently in what the town later named the Marion W. Cross School.

Marsh Fitzgerald didn't teach me his habits of mind. Being around him learnd me to examine days before yesterday for the origins of today—whether a skiing fall or, after I took to history, to study a people's past for the roots of their current politics.

My father and Charlie DeVaux learnd me vividly about consequences. "Where will the bullet stop?" is a momentous question. If you don't know the answer, you may kill someone. More, what may be the results of a word or an action—your own or another's—on the shooting range, in the voting booth, from a favor bestowed or received, in a policy, in an idea? It's a rural question with global applications.

I mourn the details of context I've omitted for the sake of brevity when writing about persons and events, although each occupied a sphere of context imprinted on my mind. For instance: the big tree under which Will Bond sprinkled his bushels of peas and beans before selling them, the cooling draft from the nearby mouth of the root cellar under his house; Charlie DeVaux describing a road for Bill and me to follow as "going up over an through" a piney ridge; the red of autumn sumacs on the path to Chink's house; snow in early spring; thin on the fields, still deep in the woods—"ass high on a tall Indian." Context was an hourly experience. It made life pleasurable and rich. It binds me to Norwich.

Will Bond, Chink, the DeVauxs, the Fitzgeralds, Miz Cross, Jack Cray, Father Hodder, so many other Norwichers, then and since, did not preach about living straight, about skill, about loyalty, about friendship, about affection. Such were not even spoken of. Nor did they imagine themselves as examples. Farthest from their minds, I suspect, was that I was being learnd.

Author Granville Austin came to live in Norwich, Vermont in 1932 at the age of five. After attending the village's primary school and then its high school, Austin graduated from Dartmouth College in Hanover, New Hampshire then earned a degree from Oxford University. He is the author of two political histories of the constitution of India, and spent some years in government service in Washington and abroad. He has held fellowships from St. Antony's College, Oxford, and the Institute of Current World Affairs. His memories of the village and people of Norwich have been his companions throughout his life, and now he has retrieved many of them for his own pleasure and that of others.

Granville Austin currenty lives with his wife in Washington, D.C.